PRESERVING

with Pomona's Pectin

UPDATED EDITION

EVEN MORE RECIPES USING THE REVOLUTIONARY
LOW-SUGAR, HIGH-FLAVOR METHOD FOR CRAFTING AND
CANNING JAMS, JELLIES, CONSERVES AND MORE

Allison Carroll Duffy

and the Partners at **Pomona's Universal Pectin®**

FAIR WINDS

Inspiring | Educating | Creating | Entertaining

Brimming with creative inspiration, how-to projects, and useful information to enrich your everyday life, Quarto Knows is a favorite destination for those pursuing their interests and passions. Visit our site and dig deeper with our books into your area of interest: Quarto Creates, Quarto Cooks, Quarto Homes, Quarto Lives, Quarto Drives, Quarto Explores, Quarto Gifts, or Quarto Kids.

Fair Winds Press titles are also available at discount for retail, wholesale, promotional, and bulk purchase. For details, contact the Special Sales Manager by email at specialsales@quarto.com or by mail at The Quarto Group, Attn: Special Sales Manager, 100 Cummings Center, Suite 265-D, Beverly, MA 01915, USA.

25 24 23 22 21   1 2 3 4 5

ISBN: 978-1-59233-993-8

Digital edition published in 2021
eISBN: 978-1-63159-983-5

Library of Congress Cataloging-in-Publication Data available.

Photography: Glenn Scott Photography
Food Styling by Alisa Neely and Natasha Taylor on pages: 172, 175, 176, 179, 183, 184, 186, and 188

Printed in China

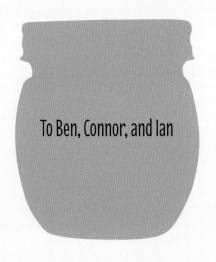

To Ben, Connor, and Ian

Contents

Preface

We, the Pomona's Universal Pectin partners, are proud to have participated with Allison Carroll Duffy in the production of this book. Allison has been a joy to work with, and the majority of the recipes come from her wonderfully creative mind and her experience preserving with Pomona's. In addition, some of the recipes come from other experienced Pomona's jam makers who answered our call for voluntary contributions of their favorite Pomona's recipes. We thank them for their generosity and willingness to share. You will find their names noted in the recipe headnotes. Allision has worked with, tested, and adapted their recipes to ensure your jam-making success.

The recipes in this book have been written exclusively for Pomona's Universal Pectin. If you try to substitute a different pectin, it won't work the same. Pomona's is a fun and easy way to preserve fruit using low amounts of any sweetener, but it differs from other pectins in how it works and how you work with it. Pomona's allows for flexibility and creativity in jam making, but it is necessary to first understand the basics of how to use it, which are well explained throughout this book.

Green Link LLC, the small family-owned business that brings you Pomona's, got its start in 1980 on a small-farm in Arlington, Washington. Farmers Brian Saunders and Connie Sumberg had an abundance of organic berries on the farm; Brian wanted to make jam and was horrified at the amount of sugar required. Some sleuthing and experimenting led to the pectin known today as Pomona's Universal Pectin. For more than twenty-five years, Connie grew the business with her sister and brother-in-law and in 2017 they retired. Casey and Sara Wolters now own and operate the business, and they are proud to continue providing this wonderful pectin.

Pomona's has been offering jam makers the happiness of healthy, homemade jams and jellies for more than thirty years. We are thrilled to provide this unique product that both brings jam making into the twenty-first century and returns us to our roots, allowing us to preserve our local fruit in a healthier (more fruity, less sugary) way. It is is a joy for us to see Pomona's and the entire whole foods movement continue to grow all across the United States and the world.

We are confident that, whether you are new to preserving with Pomona's or a seasoned expert, you will find a treasure trove of mouthwatering and compelling flavor combinations in this book.

Thank you so much for your support—and happy jamming!

Casey and Sara Wolters
The Pomona's Universal Pectin Partners

Introduction

A NEW DAY FOR JAMMING

Ah, preserving. It's safe to say that putting up fruits and vegetables when they're in season is one of the things I love to do most. And of all that I preserve, jams and jellies are my favorite. My family and I live in Maine, and we spend much of the summer and fall hunting for local fruit to transform into these preserves, which stock our pantry shelves throughout the year. We pick strawberries at a nearby farm in late June, and we buy quarts of raspberries from our neighborhood farmers' market in July. We spend warm August days picking blackberries in the woods, and we get peaches from a local orchard. Then we head up the Maine coast to a small, wild blueberry operation in late August for boxes of fresh-picked berries. Finally, in September and October we pick bushels of apples from the many old apple trees on our property. In my mind, jams and jellies are one of the best ways to preserve these fleeting summer and fall beauties, concentrating all of their glorious, fresh, heady flavors into luscious, intensely fruity and often sublime jellied concoctions—ready to be enjoyed year-round, simply by opening a jar.

Many of us have a growing interest in our food and where it comes from, and are making an effort to put more in-season, locally grown foods on our tables. Jam making, and canning and preserving in general, are enjoying a renaissance of sorts, partly due to this new mindset. Jams, jellies, and other canned goods have a long and practical history, having been produced by families in home kitchens for generations as a way to preserve the harvest for sustenance throughout the year. And while we enjoy the ease these days of not *having* to grow and preserve all of our own food, for those of us who want to eat more seasonal, locally grown, and home-produced foods, canning and preserving offer a practical way to do so.

If you are new to canning and preserving, jams and jellies are some of the best items to start with, as they are easy to can and require only a few ingredients: fruit, sweetener, sometimes an added acid like lemon juice, and pectin. When I was introduced to Pomona's Universal Pectin several years ago I was, to put it mildly, hooked. Pomona's allows you to make jams that jell reliably with low amounts of sugar (or any other sweetener you choose, such as honey, maple syrup, or stevia), which is something you cannot do with other commercial pectins. And, Pomona's contains no sugar, no preservatives, and no other added ingredients—also unlike other pectins.

My pantry shelves are stocked with rows and rows of homemade jams and jellies, and my family probably eats sixty or seventy jars per year (on toast! on yogurt! on peanut butter and jelly sandwiches!). With as much as we consume, having this kind of control over the ingredients in our jams, as only Pomona's allows, is extremely important to me. With Pomona's, I can make the full-fruit-flavored jams and jellies that my family and I love, knowing that I'm making a jam that's not only delicious but also healthful and wholesome.

In our home, jam making is a family affair, with my husband washing and de-stemming the fruit and our two young boys mashing up big bowls of berries. Sometimes a friend will stop by, or my mother will come over to help out. It's a wonderful way to spend time with family and friends—enjoying each other's company, having fun, and working together to make something wholesome, healthful, and delicious.

Whether you are a preserving beginner or an experienced canner, you're sure to find everything you need to know and more in these pages, with enough recipes to keep your pot bubbling through every season. I hope you come to enjoy your days jamming with Pomona's Pectin as much as I do mine … so let's get started!

Allison

–Allison Carroll Duffy

Chapter 1

THE BASICS

The craft of jam making has been around for centuries, and it's one of the oldest and most basic ways of preserving fruit. Originally nothing more than fruit cooked with sugar (or other ingredients where sugar wasn't available), and thickened to some degree, this jelled good has evolved a bit and taken on a variety of forms over time, but the basics remain very much the same.

What Exactly Is Jam, Anyway?

For all its varied and sometimes complex flavors, jam is actually a very simple food, containing only four primary components: fruit (or occasionally flowers, herbs, or vegetables), acid, pectin, and sweetener.

There are actually several different types of jelled products, however, and jam is just one of them, so let's get technical for a moment!

JAMS, JELLIES, PRESERVES, CONSERVES, AND MARMALADES: WHAT'S WHAT?

Jams, jellies, preserves, conserves, and marmalades are the five different types of jelled products—and they each have their own, unique characteristics. *Jam* is mashed fruit that has been jelled, whereas *jelly* is the jelled *juice* of the fruit, so it's relatively clear and contains no chunks. *Preserves* are similar to jams, but in a preserve the fruit remains more whole; small berries or cherries are left as is, and larger fruits, such as apples or peaches are cut into uniform chunks. *Conserves* are also a lot like jams, but in addition to the primary fruit, they usually contain other ingredients such as nuts or dried fruit. *Marmalades* are typically made with chopped citrus fruits and usually include some of the sliced citrus peel.

Note that for the sake of simplicity, I use the term *jam* or *jams and jellies* throughout this book when speaking about any or all of these jelled products as a group or in general.

WHAT'S THE DEAL WITH PECTIN?

Pectin is a naturally occurring substance found in varying degrees in fruit. Its sole purpose in a jam recipe is to cause the fruit to jell. Apples and citrus fruits have quite a lot of pectin, concentrated in the peel, while other fruits, such as strawberries, have very little. Originally, jams and jellies were made without adding extra pectin, relying only on the naturally occurring pectin in fruit for the jell. When pectin became commercially available, people had the option to make jam with added pectin, simplifying the jam-making process.

However, this traditional kind of pectin (whether found naturally in the fruit, homemade from apples or citrus, or purchased from the grocery or hardware store) can create a jell *only when working in conjunction with a large quantity of sugar* and the correct amount of acid. Traditional pectins that you purchase at the store may also contain dextrose (a sugar additive) and sometimes preservatives. So, as much as I value the craft of traditional jam making, neither sugar-laden, no-pectin-added jams nor the equally sugar-laden, traditional-pectin-added jams are ideal options in my book.

POMONA'S PECTIN: PURE PERFECTION!

Fortunately, Pomona's Pectin is different. It does not contain any sugar, preservatives, or other added ingredients. What it *does* contain is *low-methoxyl* citrus pectin, which means its jelling power is activated by *calcium* (which comes in a separate packet in the box with the pectin), rather than by *sugar*. With Pomona's you can sweeten your jam in almost any way, and to almost any degree, without affecting its ability to jell.

Maybe you're a big fan of honey or maple syrup over sugar. Great! With Pomona's, you can use either of those. Or perhaps you have no problem with sugar, but find most jams to be too sweet. With Pomona's, you can simply reduce the quantity of sugar to match your personal taste. Or maybe you prefer the even more subtle sweetness that fruit alone provides. In that case, unsweetened fruit juice concentrate will work like a charm for you. Other natural sweeteners, such as stevia, agave nectar, xylitol, monk fruit, and dried sugarcane juice (such as Sucanat) are also great options. If you prefer artificial sweeteners, those will work too.

The other big plus is that Pomona's is flexible. I can double or even triple a jam recipe without a problem, something that is not recommended with other pectins. And, it keeps indefinitely, which means if you don't use all the pectin you buy this year, you can continue to use it for years to come. And guess what? Making jam with Pomona's is quick and easy. So let's begin!

Let's Jam!

Jams can be so exquisite and delicious that sometimes it's hard to believe how simple they are to make. If you haven't tried canning before, like many new activities, it may appear daunting at first. Once you do it, however, you'll see how easy it is. Detailed here are the ingredients, equipment and tools, and preparation instructions you'll need to get started. You will also find the two basic methods for making jam with Pomona's Pectin and a step-by-step explanation of how to can your jam.

STEP 1: GATHER YOUR INGREDIENTS

There are a few ingredients you'll need to get started making jam. If you're feeling adventurous, you may want to try recipes with additional ingredients and flavorings, but basic jam is simple. You can make it with as few as three or four ingredients—fruit, sweetener, Pomona's Universal Pectin (and the calcium that comes with it), and in some cases acid, like lemon juice, lime juice, or vinegar.

Fruit

Fruit is the primary ingredient in most of these recipes, and you can use it in a variety of forms. A few of the recipes in this book call for flowers, herbs, or vegetables as the primary ingredient in place of fruit, and other recipes use a combination of both.

Fresh fruit is ideal, of course, but frozen and canned are fine substitutions and are certainly convenient, as the fruit is already prepped and ready to go. With either frozen or canned fruit, make sure that no sugar or other sweetener has been added to the fruit.

If using frozen fruit, you'll need to defrost, but not drain, before using (you'll use any resulting liquid along with the fruit in the recipe). You'll want to drain canned fruit, however, unless the recipe indicates otherwise. If you are making jelly, you can extract the necessary juice from the fruit itself (whether fresh, frozen, or canned), or you can use unsweetened canned or frozen juice.

Please note that I do not specify "fresh" fruit in any of the recipes, as fresh fruit is assumed. Although you may substitute unsweetened canned or frozen fruit for fresh, if a recipe specifically calls for canned or dried fruit, please do *not* substitute fresh—use canned or dried as directed.

Sweetener

As I've mentioned, one of the great things about jamming with Pomona's is that you can use any sweetener you want, in almost any quantity you want. Maple syrup, honey, agave nectar, unsweetened fruit juice concentrate, dried sugarcane juice (such as Sucanat), stevia, xylitol, monk fruit, and regular white sugar are all great options to have on hand. Artificial sweeteners will also work if that's your preference. See the sidebar below for more info about the sweeteners used in this book.

|||||||||||||||||||||||||||||||||||||||||||||||||||||||||||||||||||||||||||||||||||||||||||||||||||||||||||||||||||||||||

A NOTE ABOUT SWEETENERS

In an effort to appeal to the widest audience, the recipes in this book use commonly available sweeteners many folks enjoy—specifically sugar, honey, maple syrup, and, for an all-fruit option, unsweetened fruit juice concentrate. Additionally, some recipes use alternative sweeteners, such as stevia and monk fruit. The recipes also generally fall into the middle ground of the sweetener range suggested on the Pomona's recipe sheet that comes with every box of Pomona's Pectin.

Although with Pomona's you can use any sweetener, as well as vary the amount of sweetener, I do not recommend altering the type or quantity of sweetener called for in the recipes in this book (except as indicated in the "Customize It!" tips). These recipes have been developed and tested for safety and quality as they are written. If you'd like to try alternative or artificial sweeteners, or different amounts of sweetener, I encourage you to refer to the Pomona's recipe sheet for guidance.

|||||||||||||||||||||||||||||||||||||||||||||||||||||||||||||||||||||||||||||||||||||||||||||||||||||||||||||||||||||||||

Pomona's Universal Pectin

Each box of Pomona's Pectin includes a packet of tan pectin powder and a smaller packet of white calcium powder. The pectin is 100 percent pure low-methoxyl citrus pectin, extracted from the peel of citrus fruit. The monocalcium phosphate powder is a food-grade rock mineral source of calcium, and is necessary to activate the jelling power of the pectin. Step 4 on page 22 covers how to make calcium water with your calcium powder. Both the pectin and the calcium powder are vegan and gluten-free.

Each box of Pomona's will make two to four batches of jam, so simply store any unused pectin powder and calcium powder in a cool, dry place for later use—it will keep indefinitely.

|||||||||||||||||||||||||||||||||||||||||||||||||||||||||||||||||||||||||||||||||||||||||||||||||||||||||||||||||||||||

LOOKING FOR POMONA'S?

See Resources on page 186 for information on where you can purchase Pomona's Universal Pectin.

|||||||||||||||||||||||||||||||||||||||||||||||||||||||||||||||||||||||||||||||||||||||||||||||||||||||||||||||||||||||

Acid

Acid is a necessary element in jams and jellies for two primary reasons. First, sufficient acid allows the jam to be safely canned in a boiling water bath canner, after which it can sit on your pantry shelf and be safely consumed up to one year later. (See "Canning 101: A Few Basic Facts" on page 16 for more information.) Second, acid is sometimes necessary for the jam to jell properly. Some fruits contain enough natural acid that it's unnecessary to add more, but other fruits have slightly lower levels and therefore require that additional acid be added. Adding acid is also necessary when making jams that contain low-acid ingredients, such as vegetables, herbs, and spices. Your recipe will specify whether you need to add acid—usually lemon juice, lime juice, or vinegar.

When lemon or lime juice is specified in a recipe, you should use the bottled version rather than fresh. Yes, you read that right. I know this may come as a surprise, and frankly it's one of those things about canning that I personally find a bit challenging, but there is a very good reason for doing it this way. Bottled lemon juice and lime juice have a standard level of acidity, whereas the acidity levels of fresh lemons and fresh limes vary. Because acidity plays such an important role in jam making, it's necessary to add the proper amount, making bottled your safest option.

You'll notice there are a handful of recipes in this book that do use fresh lemon or lime juice rather than bottled, and after all this talk about the importance of bottled, you'll probably wonder why. The reason is lemons, limes, or their juices are primary *ingredients* in those recipes, not just added to increase the acid level. Any time fresh lemons or limes are called for in a recipe, it's important to use full-acid lemons or limes—Eureka and Lisbon lemons, and Tahitian (or Persian) limes, for example. Widely available, these are the standard lemons and limes that you see at most grocery stores.

If the acid called for in a recipe is vinegar, you'll need to use a vinegar with a standard level of acidity. How do you know whether the vinegar in your pantry meets this requirement? Read the label and make sure it indicates that it is diluted to 5 percent acidity. Most commercial white and apple cider vinegars will meet this criterion, but be sure to check. Do not use homemade vinegars, as you likely won't know the acid level. For more information on the importance of acid in canning, see below.

||||||||||||||||||||||||||||||||||||||||||||||||||||||||||||||||||||||||||||||||||||||||||||||||||||||||||||||||||||||||||||||||||||||||||||||||||

ACID MATTERS!

*When it comes to canning, **acid matters**. All foods fall somewhere between 0 and 14 on the pH scale, with 0 being the most acidic, and 14 being the most alkaline. For canning purposes, foods that have a pH of 4.6 or below are considered high-acid foods, whereas any food with a pH above 4.6 falls into the low-acid category. Most fruits, (though not all), are high acid, while pretty much everything else—vegetables, meats, and dairy products—are low acid. High-acid foods may be safely canned in a boiling water bath canner, a process through which the jar of food becomes shelf stable. Low-acid foods, or food mixtures that contain low-acid ingredients, can be bumped into the high-acid category with the addition of specific quantities of an acid such as lemon juice or vinegar. With the addition of acid, these foods are also suitable for canning using the boiling water bath method—dilly beans, relish, and salsa are examples. Low-acid foods that have not been further acidified, however, must be canned in a pressure canner. See "Canning 101" on page 16 for more information.*

||||||||||||||||||||||||||||||||||||||||||||||||||||||||||||||||||||||||||||||||||||||||||||||||||||||||||||||||||||||||||||||||||||||||||||||||||

Additional Ingredients

Some of the jam and jelly recipes in this book call for additional ingredients to enhance flavors. Recipes may include ground spices such as cinnamon, nutmeg, cardamom, or cayenne pepper. Or they may include fresh or whole herbs or spices, such as mint, ginger, garlic, or vanilla bean. Additionally, some savory recipes include vegetables such as peppers or onions. Wine or liqueur are called for as a flavoring in a few recipes as well. Finally, some recipes may include dried fruits, such as shredded coconut, raisins, dried cherries, or dried cranberries, as well as nuts.

When working with fresh herbs and spices, make sure they are very fresh and in good condition.

Ideally, dried fruits should be unsweetened, though a few dried fruits are difficult to find unsweetened—cranberries in particular. If you can find only the sweetened version of these, they'll do. Nuts can be used raw or roasted—just be sure they're not salted or smoked.

STEP 2: GATHER YOUR EQUIPMENT AND TOOLS

You don't need a lot of equipment to make and can jams and jellies. With the exception of a few key items, you probably have most of what you need in your kitchen already. All the recipes in this book fall into the high-acid category. This means that they can be safely canned in a boiling water bath canner, which simplifies your equipment needs a bit.

||||||||||||||||||||||||||||||||||||||||||||||||||||||||||||||||||||||||||||||||||||||||||||||||||||||||||||||||||||||||||||||||||||||||||

CANNING 101: A FEW BASIC FACTS

At its most basic, canning is the process of placing properly prepared food into clean and sterile jars, putting lids on the jars, and heat-processing the jars in a canner at a temperature hot enough and for a time long enough to kill bacteria and other microorganisms. The technical term for the latter half of this process—the actual exposure of the jars of food to the required temperature for the required amount of time in the canner—is known as processing.

There are two methods of canning suitable for the home kitchen: boiling water bath canning and pressure canning. Boiling water bath canning involves processing your jars in a boiling pot of water (212°F, or 100°C at sea level) for an allocated amount of time. This method is used for canning high-acid foods, including all of the recipes in this book. Pressure canning requires the use of a specialized piece of equipment for processing called a pressure canner, which reaches temperatures of 240°F (115°C). Pressure canning is the required method for canning low-acid foods. Why? In a word: botulism.

The bacteria that causes botulism—clostridium botulinum—likes to live in low-acid, no-oxygen environments, such as sealed jars of low-acid foods. To completely kill this bacteria, the bacteria must be exposed to a temperature of 240°F (115°C)—a temperature that only a pressure canner can achieve. Botulism-causing bacteria can't survive in a high-acid environment, however, which is why it's fine to process high-acid foods in a boiling water bath canner, even though it reaches only 212°F (100°C). These are big-picture canning concepts that are important to be aware of, which is why I mention them. However, they are not of real concern in this book because all of the recipes here are for high-acid jams and jellies, where botulism is not an issue. In fact, all the recipes in this book must be canned in a boiling water bath canner, as the high temperature reached in a pressure canner will ruin the jam's jell.

||||||||||||||||||||||||||||||||||||||||||||||||||||||||||||||||||||||||||||||||||||||||||||||||||||||||||||||||||||||||||||||||||||||||||

Boiling Water Bath Canner with Rack

A boiling water bath canner is an essential piece of equipment for canning your jams and jellies. It's pretty simple and straightforward—it's basically a large pot with a lid that has a wire rack set inside it, designed to hold filled jars in place while boiling. Boiling water bath canners are available in a handful of standard sizes and come with a rack. Basic models are not very expensive, so buying this kind of ready-to-go setup is your easiest, most convenient option. You can find them at many hardware stores, big box stores, specialty cooking stores, and online.

BOILING WATER BATH CANNER

You'll want to make sure that your canning pot is big enough so the rack will hold all of the jars that you want to process at one time without touching each other and without touching the sides of the pot. The pot also needs enough height to allow for 1 to 2 inches (2.5 to 5 cm) of water above the tops of the jars. A standard 11.5-quart (11 L) canner can accommodate 8 half-pint (236 ml) jars, while a standard 21.5-quart (20.3 L) canner will hold up to 12 half-pint (236 ml) jars. There are larger sizes available, but keep in mind that your burner needs to be powerful enough to bring your canner full of water to a rolling boil and keep it there. So, unless you have an extra-powerful stove, you'll probably want to stick with these standard-size canners, which work fine for most everyone.

Before purchasing your canner, make sure the rack it comes with is suitable for the size jars you'll be using. Some canners come with racks that have large gaps between the wires, making them better for processing pint or quart jars. If you plan to can mostly jams and jellies, which are typically canned in half-pint jars, you may want to look for a canner with a different rack—one with narrower spaces between the wires—or you may opt to buy a more suitable replacement rack. Some racks sit on the bottom of the pot, whereas other racks sit suspended inside the pot. Either option is fine so long as the rack is stable and flat—this rack is where you will set your jars for processing, and you don't want them to tip over.

CANNING RACK

"BUT MY GRANDMOTHER USED TO DO IT THAT WAY!"

*We've learned a lot about home canning over the years, and some methods, practices, and equipment that once were considered safe are no longer recommended. Here are some once-popular canning practices that you definitely should **not** do today:*

- ***Don't*** *use canning jars with wire bales and rubber gaskets, or any other old-style canning jar.*

- ***Don't*** *reuse old spaghetti sauce or salsa jars or any other jar that is not designed specifically for home canning.*

- ***Don't*** *seal jars with paraffin.*

- ***Don't*** *can using the "open kettle" method.*

- ***Don't*** *flip jars upside down after canning.*

- ***Don't*** *store your filled jars without processing first. For long-term storage (other than in the freezer), you must **always** process your jams and jellies in a boiling water bath, regardless of the sugar content of the jam.*

Jars and Lids

Use only glass, mason-style jars with two-piece metal lids designed specifically for canning. There are a handful of brands, with Ball and Kerr being two of the most popular and widely available. Many hardware stores sell canning jars, as do supermarkets, big box retailers, and specialty cooking stores. They come in several sizes, from 4 ounces (118 ml) all the way up to 64 ounces (2 L). For jams and jellies, the 8-ounce (236 ml), or half-pint, size is generally what you'll want. They're sold in cases, twelve jars to a case, and sometimes (though not always) you'll see them labeled as "Jelly Jars." They're available in either regular mouth or wide mouth, though the wide-mouth version can be difficult to find in the half-pint (236 ml) size. You can also try the 4-ounce (118 ml) jars, which are a good option if you are planning to give away your jam and jelly as gifts, as they're more of a "sample size." The recipes in this book are designed to be canned in half-pint (236 ml) jars or smaller. Therefore, jars larger than this, although great for canning other types of food, are not recommended. Additionally, jams last in the refrigerator only about three weeks once they are opened, and most of us can't polish off a pint (473 ml) or quart (946 ml) of jam that quickly!

When you buy a new case of canning jars, each jar comes with a two-piece lid, composed of the lid itself—the *dome lid*—and a screw band, which is the ring that screws around the mouth of the jar to hold the lid on. The dome lid is flat, with the exception of a small "button" in the center. This button sucks down after the jar has been properly processed and a vacuum seal has occurred. There is also

Jar

Screw Band

Dome Lid

HALF-PINT CANNING JAR, DOME LID, AND SCREW BAND

a sealant on the underside edge of the lid that helps hold the lid in place. Screw bands may be reused as long as they are rust-free and dent-free. Lids, on the other hand, cannot be reused. Fortunately, you don't have to buy a case of new jars just to get new lids. Lids, and lid-and-band combos, are sold separately, so you can replace your lids with each use, while reusing your bands and jars.

Tools, Utensils, and Additional Equipment

A stove is essential for canning, of course, and both gas and electric with the traditional coiled heating elements work well. Although it is definitely possible to can on flat-top electric stoves, and I did so successfully for several years, be aware that these types of stoves can present some challenges. Due to the nature of flat-tops and how they work, it can sometimes be difficult to keep a canner at a rolling boil, and canners can sometimes damage the burners. Flat-tops vary from one brand to the next, so it's best to check with the manufacturer to assess the suitability of your particular stove for canning.

As for the smaller stuff, standard kitchen items—pots and pans, knives, mixing bowls, and measuring cups and spoons, for example—are pretty much all you'll need for the fruit preparation and jam-making part of the process, and you probably have many of these already. Just make sure that anything that touches your jam is made of a nonreactive material. Stainless steel is ideal; food-grade plastic, heat-resistant glass or ceramic, and wood are also fine—just don't use cast iron or aluminum.

When it comes to canning-specific tools, there are all kinds of items on the market—many of which you don't need. There are, however, a handful of tools that are invaluable.

1. A *canning funnel*, also known as a *jar filler*. Wider than a typical funnel, this is ideal for getting jam into jars neatly.

2. A *jar lifter*, for lifting hot jars in and out of the canner.

3. A *headspace tool*, to make quick and accurate work of measuring the headspace in your jar.

4. A *magnetic lid wand*, for lifting hot lids out of the water before placing on filled jars.

5. A *bubble freer*, for releasing trapped air bubbles in your jam prior to putting the lids on.

CANNING TOOLS

Canning Funnel/
Jar Filler

Jar Lifter

Magnetic Lid Wand

Bubble Freer

Headspace Tool

Ladle

These items are sold individually or as part of canning tool kits, and they are all quite inexpensive. You'll find them in the canning section of hardware stores, big box stores, specialty cooking stores, and some supermarkets. See the checklist on page 20 for a complete list of jam-making and canning tools and equipment.

EQUIPMENT AND TOOL CHECKLIST
FOR JAM MAKING AND BOILING WATER BATH CANNING

Keep these tools handy, and you'll be ready to tackle any and every recipe in this book! (You won't need every tool for every recipe, of course.) And remember, anything that touches your jam or its ingredients should be made out of a nonreactive material, that is, stainless steel, wood, heat-resistant glass or ceramic, or food-grade plastic.

FOR PREP AND COOKING:

- ☐ *Assorted mixing bowls*
- ☐ *Chef's knife*
- ☐ *Paring knife*
- ☐ *Cutting board*
- ☐ *Vegetable peeler*
- ☐ *Grater (both coarse and fine)*
- ☐ *Potato masher, or other tool for mashing fruit*
- ☐ *Colander*
- ☐ *Fine mesh strainer*
- ☐ *Large slotted spoon*
- ☐ *Large mixing / cooking spoon*
- ☐ *Assorted dry and liquid measuring cups*
- ☐ *Measuring spoon set*
- ☐ *Assorted saucepans, including one small and one large with lid*
- ☐ *Heat-resistant rubber spatula*
- ☐ *Cheesecloth or jelly bag (for jelly making)*
- ☐ *Ring stand (optional—to hold jelly bag)*
- ☐ *Digital kitchen scale (optional)*

FOR CANNING:

- ☐ *Boiling water bath canner with rack*
- ☐ *Canning jars, dome lids, and screw bands*
- ☐ *Canning funnel (also called a* jar filler*)*
- ☐ *Ladle*
- ☐ *Small, clean dish cloth or paper towels*
- ☐ *Magnetic lid wand*
- ☐ *Headspace tool*
- ☐ *Bubble freer*
- ☐ *Small spoon*
- ☐ *Jar lifter*
- ☐ *Tongs*
- ☐ *Large dish towels or cooling rack*
- ☐ *Digital timer*
- ☐ *Pot holders*

STEP 3: READ YOUR RECIPE AND PREPARE YOUR EQUIPMENT AND TOOLS

There are lots of recipes in this book to choose from! Once you figure out which one you're going to make, read it all the way through before you start to be sure you have everything you need and that you fully understand the process. Because most of the recipes in this book are pretty quick to make and the process goes very quickly (you'll be lifting, filling, and capping hot jars in an assembly line sort of fashion), it's worth taking a few moments to get everything out and in place so you're working in the most efficient manner.

First, gather your jars, new lids, and screw bands. Check each jar to ensure there are no chips or cracks and check your bands to make sure they are in good condition. Then, thoroughly wash and rinse your jars, lids, and bands. Do this even when you are opening up a new box of jars, as unused jars can also be chipped or dirty. You can wash the jars and bands by hand or in the dishwasher, though lids should be washed by hand. After everything is washed, put your clean lids and bands aside for the moment.

Next, pull out your canner (make sure it's clean!) and place your clean jars on the rack in the bottom. Fill your canner about two-thirds full with water, allowing the open jars to fill with water and become completely submerged. Carefully place the canner on the stove, put the lid on, and turn the burner on high, bringing the water to a boil.

While the canner is coming to a boil, pull out any other canning tools and equipment you're going to need so that everything is within reach. This includes but is not limited to the following: jar lifter, tongs, canning funnel, ladle, headspace tool, bubble freer, small spoon, small (clean) cloth, pot holders, and a large dishcloth or cooling rack.

Once the water in the canner reaches a rolling boil (for more info, see "That's How We Roll!" on page 32), start timing, and allow boiling to continue, with the lid on, for 10 minutes. This will sterilize the jars that are in the canner. (If you are at an altitude of 1,000 feet [304.8 m] or more, you'll need to sterilize for longer. For more information, see "Adjust for Altitude!" on page 22.) Technically speaking, you don't *have* to sterilize empty jars if they will ultimately be processed in a boiling water bath canner for 10 minutes or longer. However, I always do. Because you're heating up your canner anyway, sterilizing your jars this way is easy to do, and as I see it, the cleaner the better. Once your jars are sterilized, simply turn the heat down to a low simmer and let the canner sit with the lid on. The goal is to keep the jars and the water hot until you're ready to fill the jars and process them, without all the water in the pot boiling away in the meantime. If you have the space, it's handy to keep a tea kettle of hot water on the stove throughout the jam-making process, so that you can add extra hot water to your canning pot if you need to. It's no fun when you are about to process your filled jars and realize that you don't have enough boiling water in your canner!

At some point while the canner is heating up or the jars are sterilizing, prepare your lids. Put your clean lids in a small pot, covering them with a couple of inches (5 cm) of water. Place the pot on the stove and bring the water and the lids up to a simmer. This softens the sealant around the edge of the lids. Do not boil the lids; rather, hold them at a low simmer in the pot until ready to use. Finally, place your clean bands nearby (I usually put them in a small bowl or on a dishtowel) so that they'll be easy to reach when you need them.

ADJUST FOR ALTITUDE!

At sea level, water boils at 212°F (100°C), but at higher elevations, water boils at lower temperatures. Additional sterilizing and processing times are necessary to compensate for this. The recipes in this book are written for elevations from sea level up to 999 feet (304.5 m), but if you live at a higher elevation, simply add 1 extra minute of sterilizing time and 1 extra minute of processing time for every 1,000 feet (304.8 m) above sea level. If, for example, you live at 1,300 feet (396.2 m), you'll need to sterilize and process your jars for 11 minutes (rather than 10); at 2,700 feet (823 m), you'll need 12 minutes; at 5,500 feet (1.7 km), you'll need 15 minutes; and so on. If you don't know your elevation, check with your county extension office for guidance.

STEP 4: PREPARE YOUR CALCIUM WATER AND INGREDIENTS

Once your equipment prep is taken care of, and you have your recipe and ingredients on hand, you'll want to make your calcium water (or confirm that you have enough left over from a previous batch). After that, you'll prepare your fruit and other ingredients before you hit the stove for the actual jamming part of the process.

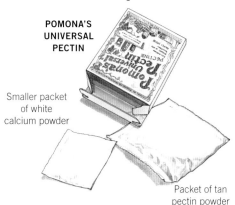

POMONA'S UNIVERSAL PECTIN

Smaller packet of white calcium powder

Packet of tan pectin powder

Preparing Your Calcium Water

As I've mentioned, every box of Pomona's Pectin contains a packet of tan pectin powder and a smaller packet of white calcium powder. The two work hand-in-hand, as the calcium activates the jelling power of the pectin.

Before making jam, use the calcium powder to make your calcium water, which you'll need for every recipe. Simply combine ½ teaspoon (1.5 g) calcium powder and ½ cup (120 ml) water in a small, clear jar with a lid. This makes enough calcium water for many batches of jam, so you won't have to do this step every time you make jam.

You can store extra calcium water in the refrigerator and use as needed, shaking before use. Refrigerated calcium water will keep for a number of months. Always examine your calcium water when you take it out of the refrigerator (before shaking it)—white sediment at the bottom of the jar is normal, but if you see any mold, scum, or discoloration, discard it and make more.

½ teaspoon (1.5 g) calcium powder

½ cup (120 ml) water

MIX UP THE CALCIUM WATER.

HOW RIPE IS RIPE?

All of the recipes in this book call for ripe fruit. However, fruits can be ripe to varying degrees, and some recipes are best made with fruit of a specific level of ripeness. In this book, if a recipe calls for a "fully ripe pear," for example, you'll want to use a pear that is ripe enough and soft enough to mash. On the other hand, if a recipe calls for a "ripe, firm pear," you'll want a pear that is ripe but still firm enough that you can cut the pear up and cook it as called for without it turning to mush. If a recipe simply calls for "ripe" fruit, any degree of ripeness is fine.

Preparing Your Fruit

If you're using fresh fruit, it should be as fresh as possible. Perhaps it goes without saying, but avoid any fruit that is overripe or diseased. Wash it thoroughly, and then remove and discard any bruised or damaged sections. Next, prepare the fruit as directed by your recipe (peeling, pitting, chopping, and so on). If you're using frozen or canned fruit, you can obviously skip all of this—simply defrost frozen fruit or drain canned fruit (unless your recipe says otherwise), and you're good to go. How you prepare your fruit from this point on will depend in large part on whether you're making a jam, jelly, preserve, conserve, or marmalade.

If you're making a jam, conserve, or marmalade, mashing the fruit is typical, though some recipes will call for chopping or dicing. For preserves, you'll want to leave the fruits whole if they are small, such as strawberries or raspberries. If your fruits are large, such as apples or peaches, cut them into uniform pieces. Some recipes require cooking the fruit during the preparation phase, while others require only mashing or chopping raw fruit. Preparation procedures will vary based on the type of fruit, type of jelled product, and the individual recipe, so be sure to refer to your recipe for specifics.

Preparing your fruit for jelly is a little different, as you'll be extracting and using the juice of the fruit, not the fruit itself. If you're using either commercially available juice for jelly or juice that you've already made in another manner (with a juicer, for example), you can, of course, skip all of the juice-making steps. If you're starting with whole fruit, however, you'll need to prepare it and juice it. First, wash your fruit and chop it up if it's large, and then, if you prefer or if the recipe calls for it, peel, core, and de-stem the fruit. You don't really need the additional pectin found in the skin and cores because you will be adding pectin. It's more work to remove the peels and cores of course, but I much prefer to do so, as it allows me to use the leftover fruit pulp for something else. There's not much I can do with the pulp after jelly making if I didn't remove the peels and cores ahead of time, other than compost it.

To extract juice from most fruits, you'll first need to cook the prepared fruit lightly with a small amount of water to make it soft enough for the juices to start flowing. Hard fruit such as apples may need as much as 1 cup (235 ml) of water per pound (455 g) of fruit, while soft, ripe fruit will need less. Juicy berries can simply be crushed to get the juices flowing. If you do choose to cook them, ⅛ cup (28 ml) of water per pound (455 g) should be plenty—and sometimes you'll need even less. Knowing exactly how much water to cook fruit with can be a little tricky because, depending on the type of fruit and the degree of ripeness, natural juiciness will vary. Ideally, you want to add just enough water so the fruit will yield the required amount of juice for your recipe. The more water you add to the fruit, the more diluted your juice (and the jelly you make from it) will be, yet adding some amount of water is essential for most fruits. Although it's never an exact science, the recipes in this book specify water quantities and cooking times that will yield pretty close to the correct quantity of juice for your jelly, so always refer to your recipe.

After you've cooked your fruit (if necessary) to make it soft, mash it and transfer it to a damp jelly bag or layered cheesecloth. (For more on using jelly bags and cheesecloth, see opposite page.) Hang the bag over a bowl and allow the juice to drip into the bowl until the dripping stops—at least two hours, and often longer.

If you are making a jelly with flowers or herbs, you'll steep the flowers or herbs in hot water or another hot liquid and then strain them with a jelly bag, cheesecloth, or a fine mesh strainer, discarding the flowers and herbs and reserving the infused liquid. As always, remember to refer to your recipe for specific ingredient prep requirements.

WHAT'S A JELLY BAG, ANYWAY?

Jelly is made from the juice of the fruit (or, in some cases, flower or herb-infused liquid), so to make jelly you need a way to extract the juice or liquid from the fruit or plant. A jelly bag—which is essentially a cloth bag—makes this process convenient. To use it, simply dampen the bag and pour your crushed fruit or plant matter, plus any infused liquid, into it. Then suspend the bag over a bowl, allowing the liquid to drip out of the bag into the bowl. Discard the contents of the bag (or use them for another purpose) after draining, reserving the juice or liquid for your jelly. For added convenience, you can buy a ring stand, which is a simple metal stand designed to hold the jelly bag while it's dripping.

For a less expensive and equally effective alternative, use a large piece of cheesecloth, folded over itself a few times, to fashion your own jelly bag. Simply place your fruit on the dampened, layered cloth, gather the cloth up around the fruit, tie it at the top or secure it with an elastic band, and hang it up to drip with a bowl underneath. After you're done, wash your cheesecloth well, let it air-dry, fold it up and store it in a clean, dry place, and use it again next time you make jelly.

JELLY BAG AND RING STAND

CHEESECLOTH JELLY BAG SET-UP

MEASURING UP!

Because individual fruits of the same kind can vary so much in size, for the sake of accuracy, most of the recipes in this book call for fruit by weight. If you're planning to do a lot of jam making, a digital kitchen scale is an excellent investment. There are relatively inexpensive models available (around twenty dollars), and with a scale at your disposal, you'll know you're using the correct amount of fruit in your recipe. If you don't have a scale at home, weighing your fruit when you purchase it at the grocery store or farmers' market is another good option.

That said, there are times when weighing just isn't an option. If you're itching to make jam but don't have a scale handy, the following chart will help you determine how much fruit you'll need for different recipes in this book. Keep in mind the quantities are approximate, and may vary based on the size of the fruit.

FRUIT (fresh)	WEIGHT (1 pound = 455 g)	UNIT OR VOLUME EQUIVALENT
Apples	*1 pound*	*3 medium apples*
Apricots	*1 pound*	*5 to 8 medium apricots*
Blackberries	*1 pound*	*3½ cups whole blackberries*
Blueberries	*1 pound*	*4 cups blueberries*
Cherries (sweet)	*1 pound*	*3 cups whole cherries*
Figs	*1 pound*	*13 to 14 small to medium figs*
Grapes (sweet)	*1 pound*	*3 cups whole large grapes*
Grapefruits	*1 pound*	*1 to 2 medium grapefruits*
Kiwis	*1 pound*	*5 to 6 medium kiwis*
Lemons	*1 pound*	*4 to 6 medium lemons*
Limes	*1 pound*	*5 to 8 medium limes*
Mangoes	*1 pound*	*2 small mangoes*
Nectarines	*1 pound*	*3 medium nectarines*
Oranges	*1 pound*	*2 to 3 medium oranges*
Peaches	*1 pound*	*3 medium peaches*
Pears	*1 pound*	*3 small to medium pears*
Plums (sweet)	*1 pound*	*4 to 6 medium plums*
Raspberries	*1 pound*	*2 (level) pints*
Rhubarb	*1 pound trimmed*	*4 to 8 stalks, or 3½ to 4 cups medium dice*
Strawberries	*1 pound*	*1 (level) quart, whole*

Preparing Additional Ingredients

Along with a recipe's primary ingredients, many recipes include additional, supporting ingredients such as herbs, spices, vegetables, nuts, or dried fruit. These ingredients may be prepared in a variety of ways, so refer to your recipe for specifics.

STEP 5: COOK YOUR JAM

Once you've prepared your fruit, you're ready to hit the stove—almost. Before you do, make sure you're working with the correct amount of prepared fruit. After you've prepared your fruit as called for in your recipe, you will (for most recipes) need to measure out a specific quantity of prepared fruit. After measuring out the correct quantity, you may have a little bit left over, but that's normal—simply save it for another use, or compost it, if you prefer. Whatever you do, be sure that you proceed with the exact quantity of prepared fruit that the recipe calls for. This is important because recipes call for specific amounts of pectin to jell specific quantities of fruit. If you use more or less fruit mixture than the recipe calls for, your jam may not jell properly. Additionally, the end product may not contain the proper level of acidity.

Now you're ready for the last part of the process. There are a couple of different ways you can use Pomona's Pectin to make jams and jellies. The method you use will depend on the type of jam you're making.

Pomona's Primary Method: Cooked Jam with Low Sugar or Honey

The primary method used in this book is the cooked jam with low sugar or honey method. It's extremely versatile, and will accommodate many different types and quantities of sweetener, including alternative natural sweeteners that measure like sugar and alternative natural sweeteners that measure like honey, as well as artificial sweeteners that measure like sugar. It's easy, too! Following is what you do.

1. Pour your prepared, measured fruit or fruit juice into a large saucepan, and then add your measured amount of lemon juice (or lime juice or vinegar), if your recipe calls for it, and your measured calcium water.

Calcium water

Lemon juice

ADD LEMON JUICE (IF CALLED FOR) AND CALCIUM WATER TO PREPARED FRUIT.

2. In a separate bowl, combine your measured amounts of sweetener and Pomona's pectin powder. Mix thoroughly and set aside. (Note that there are two recipes in this book—both pepper jellies—where this step is done differently. In those two cases, please follow the directions provided to properly mix your pectin into your sweetener.)

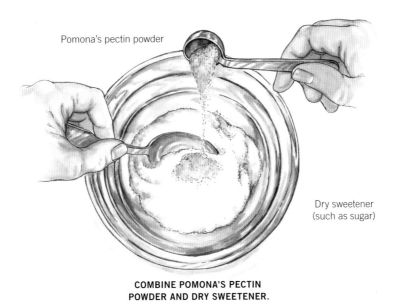

Pomona's pectin powder

Dry sweetener
(such as sugar)

**COMBINE POMONA'S PECTIN
POWDER AND DRY SWEETENER.**

or

Pomona's pectin powder

Liquid sweetener
(such as honey)

**COMBINE POMONA'S PECTIN
POWDER AND LIQUID SWEETENER.**

3. Bring prepared, measured fruit mixture to a full boil (for more information, see "That's How We Roll!" on page 32).

4. Add the pectin-sweetener mixture to the boiling fruit mixture, stir well for 1 to 2 minutes to dissolve the pectin while the mixture returns to a full boil, and then remove it from the heat.

Measured quantity of sweetener and pectin

Boiling fruit (or fruit juice) mixture

**ADD THE PECTIN-SWEETENER MIXTURE
TO THE BOILING FRUIT MIXTURE.**

And that's it! You now have a jam or jelly that's ready for canning.

Pomona's Fruity Alternative: Cooked, All-Fruit Jam

If you want to make jam that is even less sweet, an all-fruit jam is a great option. Jams made with this method consist entirely of fruit, sweetened only with unsweetened fruit juice concentrate such as apple juice concentrate, orange juice concentrate, or white grape juice concentrate. There are a handful of recipes in this book that use this method. The biggest difference between the primary cooked jam with low-sugar or honey method and the alternate all-fruit method is that in the primary method, you can simply mix your sweetener and the pectin together in a bowl, whereas with the all-fruit method, you have to heat up the sweetener (the fruit juice concentrate) and then use a blender or food processor to thoroughly dissolve the Pomona's pectin powder in the juice before adding it to the boiling fruit mixture. It takes an extra step or two, but it's still easy. Here's what you do:

1. Pour your prepared, measured fruit into a large saucepan, and then add your measured amount of lemon juice (or lime juice), if your recipe calls for it, and your measured amount of calcium water.

2. In a separate saucepan, bring your measured amount of fruit juice concentrate to a boil.

3. Pour hot juice concentrate into a blender or food processor; then add pectin powder. Vent the lid and blend for 1 to 2 minutes, stopping to scrape down sides as necessary, until pectin is dissolved.

4. Bring fruit mixture to a full boil (for more information, see "That's How We Roll!" on page 32), and then stir in the hot pectin-concentrate mixture. Continue to cook and stir for 1 minute while the mixture returns to a full boil, and then remove from heat.

Now your jam is ready for canning!

THAT'S HOW WE ROLL!

*We all know what a boil is, but when it comes to jam making and canning, a **rolling** boil—or a **full** boil, as I often call it—is what really counts. A rolling boil and a full boil are essentially the same thing, but I tend to use the term **rolling boil** when I'm referring to the water in the canner, while I usually use the term **full boil** when I'm talking about the jam. So what **is** a rolling boil or a full boil? It's **not** when the bubbling first starts. Rather, it's rolling in a major way, meaning that the liquid is really bubbling hard—not just a little bit. When jars are in the canner for processing or sterilizing, the water in the canner needs to be at a rolling boil before you start the sterilizing or processing time. Also, jam should be at a full boil before you add the pectin to ensure that the pectin dissolves thoroughly. If your jam's boil can be stirred down, it's not a full boil; just wait a few moments for things to really get rolling!*

STEP 6: CAN YOUR JAM

Once your jam is done, it's time to get it in the can—or rather, the jars. Don't worry if your jam looks a bit soupy at this point because this is normal; jam doesn't fully jell until after canning *and* after it's completely cool. Assuming you've followed all the previous steps, you're ready to can.

Filling Your Jars

It's important that both the jam and the jars are hot when filling the jars, so once you start canning, you'll want to move promptly so they don't cool off. Follow these steps and you'll have smooth sailing:

1. Take the lid off the canner. Use the jar lifter or tongs to remove one hot, sterilized jar at a time, dumping the water out of the jar and back into the canner as you go. Place hot, empty jars on a clean dish towel or cooling rack on the counter. No need to dry the jars—it's okay if they are wet. Once all the jars are removed, place the lid back on the canner and crank the heat up so that the water can return to a boil while you're filling your jars.

2. Using the ladle and the canning funnel, ladle hot jam into each jar, being careful not to overfill the jars. If you need to pick up or move the jars, don't forget to use a large pot holder or dish cloth—these jars are hot!

LADLE HOT JAM INTO HOT JARS.

3. Stick the bubble freer down into the jam all the way to the bottom of the jar, hold the bubble freer flat against the inside edge of the jar, and then gently run it all the way around the inside edge of each jar to release any trapped air bubbles.

REMOVE AIR BUBBLES FROM JAM WITH BUBBLE FREER.

4. Using the headspace tool, measure the headspace of each jar. The headspace is the distance between the top of the jam and the top rim of the jar. To measure it, simply hold the headspace tool very gently on the surface of the jam, against the inside rim of the jar, and measure the distance from the surface of the jam to the very top of the jar. Most jam and jelly recipes call for ¼ inch (6 mm) of headspace, though always check your recipe. Using a small spoon, add or remove jam from each jar as necessary to achieve the proper headspace, remeasuring if needed. If you don't have enough jam to completely fill your last jar, simply refrigerate that jar after cooling and enjoy right away (rather than processing it).

¼ inch (6 mm)—proper headspace for jams and jellies

MEASURE THE HEADSPACE USING THE HEADSPACE TOOL.

5. Carefully wipe the top rim of each jar with a clean, damp cloth or paper towel to remove any jam. This is where the lid meets the jar—ensuring that it's clean will help achieve a good seal.

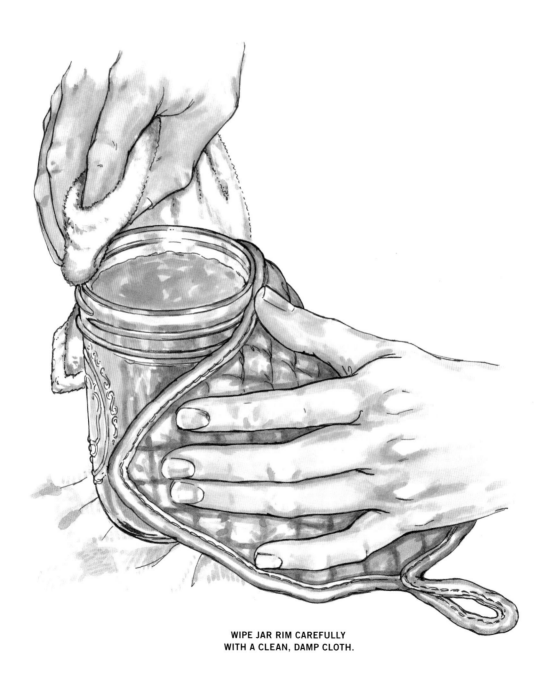

**WIPE JAR RIM CAREFULLY
WITH A CLEAN, DAMP CLOTH.**

6. Using the magnetic lid wand, remove the lids one at a time from the simmering water in the small pot (the lids will be wet, but there's no need to dry them), and center a lid on the top of each jar. Gently place a screw band down over each lid and screw the band onto the jar until you meet resistance—and then tighten just a tiny bit more. This is known as *fingertip tight*. Do not overtighten the bands, as air needs to escape from the jar during processing.

CENTER LID ON TOP OF JAR USING THE MAGNETIC LID WAND.

GENTLY SCREW BAND ONTO JAR, UNTIL FINGERTIP TIGHT.

Loading the Canner

Remove the lid from the canner, and, using the jar lifter, gently lower each jar down into the boiling water and place it on the rack in the canner. (If the boiling water is making it hard to see, you can turn the heat down temporarily as you're placing the jars.) Ideally, you'll want to hold the jars by their bodies, not by their necks, so that you don't dislodge the lids and the screw bands. Be careful not to let the jars tip over—and if they do, right them immediately. Also, make sure the jars are not touching each other, or the sides of the canner, and that there is at least 1 to 2 inches (2.5 to 5 cm) of water covering all of the jars. This allows water to circulate freely and thoroughly around all parts of every jar during processing, which will ensure that the jam is subject to the temperature necessary to kill any microorganisms. If, after you've placed your jars in the canner, you find that they are not covered sufficiently with water, add more hot water to the canner as needed.

LOWER FILLED JARS INTO BOILING WATER USING THE JAR LIFTER.

INTERIOR VIEW OF LOADED CANNER. Make sure jars are upright, not touching each other or the sides of the canner, and are covered by at least 1 to 2 inches (2.5 to 5 cm) of water.

Processing Your Jars in the Canner

After you've loaded the canner, place the lid on it, crank the heat up to high, and bring the water to a rolling boil (for more information, see "That's How We Roll!" on page 32). Once the water is at a rolling boil, you can start your processing time. Set your timer for the specific processing time indicated in your recipe—usually 10 minutes for jams and jellies, but always double-check. If you're at 1,000 feet (304.8 m) or more of elevation, you'll need to increase your processing time (see "Adjust for Altitude!" on page 24 for more information). After the processing is complete, turn off the heat, and allow the canner and jars to sit—untouched—for 5 minutes. This 5-minute waiting period is important. If you remove your jars from the canner immediately, jam will sometimes seep out of them—an occurrence known as siphoning—due to the dramatic change in temperature and pressure. The 5-minute waiting period allows the jam to cool down enough before coming out of the canner that siphoning is unlikely to occur. Be sure that you don't wait longer than 5 minutes, however, as exposure to heat for too long a period may cause your jam not to jell properly.

|||||||||||||||||||||||||||||||||||||||||||||||||||||||||||||||||||||||||||||||||||||||||||||||||||||||||||||||||||||||

WHAT'S ALL THAT RACKET IN THERE?

During processing, there's a lot going on in your canning pot. Boiling water circulates around the jars, heating them to the required temperature (212°F [100°C] at sea level for boiling water bath canning) and exposing the food in the jars to that temperature for the specified processing time. As the food heats up it expands, forcing air out of the jars. After processing, when the jars begin to cool, the food shrinks, and, because the air was forced out of the jars during processing, when the food shrinks, the lids get sucked down. This creates a vacuum seal, which will keep out contaminants and allow the sealed jar of food to be safely stored at room temperature.

|||||||||||||||||||||||||||||||||||||||||||||||||||||||||||||||||||||||||||||||||||||||||||||||||||||||||||||||||||||||

Removing Your Jars from the Canner

After the canner has cooled for 5 minutes, it's time to remove the jars. Using the jar lifter, carefully lift the jars from the canner one at a time, always keeping them upright, and place them on a dish towel or cooling rack on the counter, with space in between each jar. There will likely be a small pool of water on the top of each jar when you take it out, but don't worry about that—the water will evaporate as the jar cools. It's tempting to check out your jam, move the jars around, and handle the jars in general, but refrain! This cooling period is when your jars are in the process of sealing, and the less you handle your jars during this time, the more likely you are to get a proper seal. Allow your jars to cool, untouched, for 12 to 24 hours. You sometimes (though not always) will hear little popping noises as the jars cool—don't worry. This popping is a good thing! It's the little "button" on the top of the lid sucking down, and it's usually a good indication that a jar is in the process of sealing.

Checking Your Seals and Storing Your Jars

After your jars have cooled for at least 12 hours, you'll want to check them to ensure that each jar has sealed properly. To do this, press gently with your finger into the center of each lid. If the "button" that is in the center of each lid is already depressed, and there is no movement when you press down, then you have a proper vacuum seal. If the "button" is *not* depressed, and there is movement when you press on it, then your jar did not seal properly.

If a jar doesn't seal (which occasionally does happen), you have a couple of options. You may want to re-can your jam, though this is the most labor-intensive option. To do this, you'll need to dump out the jar, reheat the jam to boiling, and reprocess it in a clean, hot jar with a new lid for the recommended amount of time. I tend to go for an easier option—if I'm planning on eating it right away, I'll put it in the refrigerator. It will keep this way for about 3 weeks. Or, if I'm looking for longer-term storage, I'll freeze the jam, as it will keep in the freezer for about 6 months. Freezing it right in the jar is just fine, though make sure the jam is cool first, and be sure to remove the lid and take out a couple of spoonfuls so that there is at least ½ inch (1.3 cm) of headspace before re-capping and freezing. This will allow room for the jam to expand when it freezes.

CHECK FOR A PROPER SEAL.

Fortunately, jars do seal properly most of the time. After you've confirmed that your jars have sealed, remove the screw bands. (You'll notice that the bands are already quite loose—this is normal!) It may seem counter-intuitive to take the bands off, but at this point, each lid is adhering to the jar because of the vacuum seal; the screw bands are no longer doing anything useful and can cause various problems during storage if left on. After removing the screw bands, wash them, thoroughly dry them, and then store them for future use. (It's helpful to keep bands nearby, so you can easily reach for one to put on after opening a jar, or when giving a jar as a gift!) Then, rinse the outside of your sealed jars thoroughly to remove any jam that may have gotten on the outside of the jar during filling or processing. Dry your jars, clearly label and date them, and store them—preferably in a clean, dry, dark location between 50 and 70°F (10 to 21°C). Your sealed jars of jam will keep well this way for up to one year.

THIS JAR *IS* SEALED PROPERLY—
THE "BUTTON" IS DOWN.

THIS JAR *IS NOT* SEALED PROPERLY—
THE "BUTTON" IS UP.

Before you open up a jar that has been stored, it's always a good idea to make sure the jar is still vacuum sealed. To do this, check that the button in the center is still depressed, and, with your fingers, very gently try to pull up the lid, making sure that it doesn't budge. You'll also want to visually inspect the jam. If you notice any obvious signs of spoilage, discard immediately. If your jar was processed correctly, it should be fine, but seal failures and spoilage occasionally do occur during storage, so it's always important to check.

You may notice when you're examining your jar that the jam has separated, but don't be alarmed—this is normal for many jams and is not a sign of spoilage. When you open a jar of jam that has separated, simply mix it up well. Opening up a properly vacuum-sealed jar typically requires more than hands alone— I use a butter knife or other metal kitchen utensil to carefully pry lids off. After you open one of your jars of jam, store it in the refrigerator, capped with a lid and a screw band. It will keep this way for about three weeks.

Making Pomona's Your Own

We all have individual tastes of course, and as I see it, that's a beautiful thing. My hope is that this book will appeal to folks from across the spectrum—new and experienced jam makers alike, with a wide variety of personal preferences. At the beginning of each chapter, I've included a few classic recipes—"Simple Classics," I call them—that are very easy to make. If you're new to jam making, or simply enjoy classic flavors, these recipes are a great place to start. There are also some fairly complex, out-of-the-box recipes that I hope will appeal to more experienced jammers and those with adventurous tastes. In addition, I've included tips throughout the book on specific ways you can customize certain recipes.

For safety and quality reasons, I do not recommend changing the recipes in this book in any ways other than what I suggest. However, if you are interested in customizing your jams more extensively, I encourage you to refer to the recipe insert sheet in your box of Pomona's Pectin for guidance. That said, I've tried hard to develop a diverse selection of recipes for this book—my family and I really enjoy them, and I truly hope you love them just as much as we do.

Happy Jamming!

Chapter 2

JAMS

Jams are the workhorses of jelled goods. Nothing more than mashed or chopped fruit that's been lightly sweetened and jelled by pectin, they are the simplest of all to make. Jams are incredibly practical and versatile, too—I use them on peanut butter and jam sandwiches, in smoothies, in hot cereal, on toast, on yogurt, on granola, on ice cream, in cookies, and in pies … you get the idea. Jams are humble and unassuming and yet, extraordinarily delicious.

SIMPLE CLASSIC: BLUEBERRY JAM

Here in Maine, we're fortunate that blueberries are abundant in late summer, and I never tire of this classic way to enjoy them. Blueberries require very little prep, and this jam has few ingredients, so it's easy and quick to prepare, making it an excellent choice for new jam makers. A dollop of this luscious, deep blue jam on a muffin is scrumptious—or, try it on a cracker with some extra-sharp cheddar for an unexpected flavor treat.

2¼ pounds (1 kg) blueberries*

¼ cup (60 ml) lemon juice

2 teaspoons (10 ml) calcium water**

1 cup (200 g) sugar

2 teaspoons (6 g) Pomona's pectin powder

Not sure how much fruit to purchase? See "Measuring Up!" on page 26.

**For information on how to prepare calcium water, refer to page 22.*

1. If you are new to canning, or need a refresher, refer to chapter 1 (pages 12–41) for step-by-step guidance and additional information on how to safely can your jam. Once ready, proceed as follows.
2. Prepare your jars, lids, and bands; heat up your canner; and sterilize your jars.
3. Rinse blueberries, remove stems, and mash in a large bowl.
4. Measure 4 cups (946 ml) of mashed blueberries (saving any extra for another use), and combine the measured quantity in a saucepan with lemon juice and calcium water. Mix well.
5. In a separate bowl, combine sugar and pectin powder. Mix thoroughly and set aside.
6. Bring blueberry mixture to a full boil over high heat. Slowly add pectin-sugar mixture, stirring constantly. Continue to stir vigorously for 1 to 2 minutes to dissolve pectin while the jam comes back up to a boil. Once the jam returns to a full boil, remove it from the heat.
7. **Can Your Jam:** Remove jars from canner and ladle jam into hot jars, leaving ¼ inch (6 mm) of headspace. Remove trapped air bubbles, wipe rims with a damp cloth, put on lids and screw bands, and tighten to fingertip tight. Lower filled jars into canner, ensuring jars are not touching each other and are covered with at least 1 to 2 inches (2.5 to 5 cm) of water. Place lid on canner, return to a rolling boil, and process for 10 minutes (adjusting for altitude if necessary). Turn off heat and allow canner to sit untouched for 5 minutes, then remove jars and allow to cool undisturbed for 12 to 24 hours. Confirm that jars have sealed, then store properly.

YIELD: 4 TO 5 HALF-PINT (8-OUNCE, OR 236 ML) JARS

CUSTOMIZE IT!

If you're looking for something new, try spicing it up! At the same time that you add the calcium water, add up to 1 teaspoon (2.5 g) of ground ginger, cardamom, cloves, cinnamon, nutmeg, or allspice. Or, you can mix and match these spices—just be sure that the total spice quantity does not exceed 1 teaspoon (2.5 g).

SIMPLE CLASSIC: APRICOT JAM

Apricots fresh from the tree on a warm summer day are one of the world's true wonders. Well, perhaps that's overstating it a bit, but they certainly come close, in my mind anyway. This lovely little fruit tastes amazing unadorned, and this recipe is suitably simple, so it's ideal for beginning jam makers. Spread on a slice of pound cake, or for a special treat, use it as a filling between layers of a cake!

2½ pounds (1.1 kg) fully ripe apricots*

¼ cup (60 ml) lemon juice

4 teaspoons (20 ml) calcium water**

1½ cups (300 g) sugar

3 teaspoons (9 g) Pomona's pectin powder

Not sure how much fruit to purchase? See "Measuring Up!" on page 26.

**For information on how to prepare calcium water, refer to page 22.*

1. If you are new to canning, or need a refresher, refer to chapter 1 (pages 12–41) for step-by-step guidance and additional information on how to safely can your jam. Once ready, proceed as follows.
2. Prepare your jars, lids, and bands; heat up your canner; and sterilize your jars.
3. Rinse apricots, remove stems, and then slice in half or pull apart. Remove pits, chop apricots into small pieces, and mash in a large bowl. (For more information, see "To Peel or Not to Peel?" on page 76.)
4. Measure 4 cups (946 ml) of mashed apricots (saving any extra for another use), and combine measured quantity in a saucepan with lemon juice and calcium water. Mix well.
5. In a separate bowl, combine sugar and pectin powder. Mix thoroughly and set aside.
6. Bring apricot mixture to a full boil over high heat. Slowly add pectin-sugar mixture, stirring constantly. Continue to stir vigorously for 1 to 2 minutes to dissolve pectin while the jam comes back up to a boil. Once the jam returns to a full boil, remove it from the heat.
7. **Can Your Jam:** Remove jars from canner and ladle jam into hot jars, leaving ¼ inch (6 mm) of headspace. Remove trapped air bubbles, wipe rims with a damp cloth, put on lids and screw bands, and tighten to fingertip tight. Lower filled jars into canner, ensuring jars are not touching each other and are covered with at least 1 to 2 inches (2.5 to 5 cm) of water. Place lid on canner, return to a rolling boil, and process for 10 minutes (adjusting for altitude if necessary). Turn off heat and allow canner to sit untouched for 5 minutes, then remove jars and allow to cool undisturbed for 12 to 24 hours. Confirm that jars have sealed, then store properly.

YIELD: 4 TO 5 HALF-PINT (8-OUNCE, OR 236 ML) JARS

CUSTOMIZE IT!

If you're looking for something new, why not try different fruits? In place of or in combination with the apricot in this recipe, use sweet cherry, pear, mango, peach, fig, or sweet plum—or use a combination of any of these fruits.

APRICOT ANGST

Trying to mash rock-hard apricots is really not a lot of fun, so be sure that your apricots are fully ripe and soft enough to mash before beginning. If they're not, however, simply place pitted, chopped apricots in a saucepan with ¼ cup (60 ml) water (or slightly more if necessary). Simmer for 5 minutes to soften them, and then mash. (There's no need to drain the water after cooking—simply mash the apricot mixture as is.)

SIMPLE CLASSIC: STRAWBERRY JAM

Classics are often classics for a reason, and this strawberry jam is a great example—when you're working with perfectly ripe, in-season fruit, you don't have to add much to make a spectacular jam. Use locally grown berries if you can, as their flavor and color will be richer and more vibrant than the grocery store variety. This is an excellent recipe to start with if you're new to jam making. For something different, try it warmed on top of pancakes—delicious!

2¼ pounds (1 kg) strawberries*

2 teaspoons (10 ml) calcium water**

1 cup (200 g) sugar

2 teaspoons (6 g) Pomona's pectin powder

Not sure how much fruit to purchase? See "Measuring Up!" on page 26.

**For information on how to prepare calcium water, refer to page 22.*

1. If you are new to canning, or need a refresher, refer to chapter 1 (pages 12–41) for step-by-step guidance and additional information on how to safely can your jam. Once ready, proceed as follows.
2. Prepare your jars, lids, and bands; heat up your canner; and sterilize your jars.
3. Rinse strawberries, remove stems, and mash in a large bowl.
4. Measure 4 cups (946 ml) of mashed strawberries (saving any extra for another use), and combine the measured quantity in a saucepan with calcium water. Mix well.
5. In a separate bowl, combine sugar and pectin powder. Mix thoroughly and set aside.
6. Bring strawberry mixture to a full boil over high heat. Slowly add pectin-sugar mixture, stirring constantly. Continue to stir vigorously for 1 to 2 minutes to dissolve pectin while the jam comes back up to a boil. Once the jam returns to a full boil, remove it from the heat.
7. **Can Your Jam:** Remove jars from canner and ladle jam into hot jars, leaving ¼ inch (6 mm) of headspace. Remove trapped air bubbles, wipe rims with a damp cloth, put on lids and screw bands, and tighten to fingertip tight. Lower filled jars into canner, ensuring jars are not touching each other and are covered with at least 1 to 2 inches (2.5 to 5 cm) of water. Place lid on canner, return to a rolling boil, and process for 10 minutes (adjusting for altitude if necessary). Turn off heat and allow canner to sit untouched for 5 minutes, then remove jars and allow to cool undisturbed for 12 to 24 hours. Confirm that jars have sealed, then store properly.

YIELD: 4 TO 5 HALF-PINT (8-OUNCE, OR 236 ML) JARS

CUSTOMIZE IT!

If you're looking for something new, why not try different fruits? In place of or in combination with the strawberry in this recipe, or in the All-Fruit Strawberry Jam (opposite) use kiwi, currant, raspberry, gooseberry, sour blackberry, sour cherry, sour plum, or canned pineapple—or use a combination of any of these fruits.

ALL-FRUIT STRAWBERRY JAM

I make this jam more than any other jam, hands down. My two young boys eat peanut butter and jam sandwiches nonstop it seems, and because I like to keep their sugar intake in check, this is my go-to choice. It's sweetened only with fruit juice concentrate, so it's about as close as you can get to just fruit in a jam, and it's loaded with fantastic, fresh strawberry flavor.

1¾ pounds (800 g) strawberries*

2 teaspoons (10 ml) calcium water**

1 cup (235 ml) unsweetened white grape juice concentrate

2 teaspoons (6 g) Pomona's pectin powder

*Not sure how much fruit to purchase? See "Measuring Up!" on page 26.

**For information on how to prepare calcium water, refer to page 22.

1. If you are new to canning, or need a refresher, refer to chapter 1 (pages 12–41) for step-by-step guidance and additional information on how to safely can your jam. Once ready, proceed as follows.
2. Prepare your jars, lids, and bands; heat up your canner; and sterilize your jars.
3. Rinse strawberries, remove stems, and mash in a large bowl.
4. Measure 3 cups (710 ml) of mashed strawberries (saving any extra for another use), and combine the measured quantity in a saucepan with calcium water. Mix well.
5. In a separate pan, bring white grape juice concentrate to a boil. Pour hot juice concentrate into a blender or food processor, and then add pectin powder. Vent the lid and blend for 1 to 2 minutes, stopping to scrape down sides with a rubber spatula as needed, until powder is thoroughly dissolved. Set aside.
6. Bring strawberries to a full boil over high heat, and then slowly add the pectin–juice concentrate mixture, stirring constantly. Continue to cook and stir jam for 1 minute as the jam comes back up to a boil. Once the jam returns to a full boil, remove it from the heat.
7. **Can Your Jam:** Remove jars from canner and ladle jam into hot jars, leaving ¼ inch (6 mm) of headspace. Remove trapped air bubbles, wipe rims with a damp cloth, put on lids and screw bands, and tighten to fingertip tight. Lower filled jars into canner, ensuring jars are not touching each other and are covered with at least 1 to 2 inches (2.5 to 5 cm) of water. Place lid on canner, return to a rolling boil, and process for 10 minutes (adjusting for altitude if necessary). Turn off heat and allow canner to sit untouched for 5 minutes, then remove jars and allow to cool undisturbed for 12 to 24 hours. Confirm that jars have sealed, then store properly.

YIELD: 4 HALF-PINT (8-OUNCE, OR 236 ML) JARS

STIR IT UP!

Strawberry jam often separates after canning, so be sure to mix it well before serving.

ALL-FRUIT CHERRY-PEACH JAM

Cherries and peaches are so naturally sweet that they're especially suitable for an all-fruit jam. For the sweetest, most delicious jam, select peaches and cherries that are at peak ripeness, and be sure to choose a sweet cherry variety—Bing cherries are a good option. This jam is so intensely fruity that you'll be hard-pressed not to eat it by the spoonful right out of the jar. It's also delicious swirled into a bowl of yogurt.

1 pound (455 g) fully ripe peaches*

1 pound (455 g) sweet cherries*

¼ cup (60 ml) lemon juice

4 teaspoons (20 ml) calcium water**

1 cup (235 ml) unsweetened apple juice concentrate

3 teaspoons (9 g) Pomona's pectin powder

*Not sure how much fruit to purchase? See "Measuring Up!" on page 26.

**For information on how to prepare calcium water, refer to page 22.

1. If you are new to canning, or need a refresher, refer to chapter 1 (pages 12–41) for step-by-step guidance and additional information on how to safely can your jam. Once ready, proceed as follows.

2. Prepare your jars, lids, and bands; heat up your canner; and sterilize your jars.

3. Peel and remove pits from peaches, and then mash the peaches in a large bowl. Set aside. (For more information, see "How to Skin a Peach" on page 58.)

4. Rinse cherries, remove stems, slice in half and remove pits, and then chop the cherries—by hand with a chef's knife or with a food processor. (For more information, see "Painless Pitting" on page 70.)

5. Combine the mashed peaches and the chopped cherries and mix well. Measure 3 cups (710 ml) of the fruit mixture (saving any extra for another use), and combine the measured quantity in a saucepan with lemon juice and calcium water. Mix well.

6. In a separate pan, bring apple juice concentrate to a boil. Pour hot juice concentrate into a blender or food processor, and then add pectin powder. Vent the lid and blend for 1 to 2 minutes, stopping to scrape down sides with a rubber spatula as needed, until powder is thoroughly dissolved. Set aside.

7. Bring cherry-peach mixture to a full boil over high heat, and then slowly add the pectin–juice concentrate mixture, stirring constantly. Continue to cook and stir jam for 1 minute as the jam comes back up to a boil. Once the jam returns to a full boil, remove it from the heat.

8. **Can Your Jam:** Remove jars from canner and ladle jam into hot jars, leaving ¼ inch (6 mm) of headspace. Remove trapped air bubbles, wipe rims with a damp cloth, put on lids and screw bands, and tighten to fingertip tight. Lower filled jars into canner, ensuring jars are not touching each other and are covered with at least 1 to 2 inches (2.5 to 5 cm) of water. Place lid on canner, return to a rolling boil, and process for 10 minutes (adjusting for altitude if necessary). Turn off heat and allow canner to sit untouched for 5 minutes, then remove jars and allow to cool undisturbed for 12 to 24 hours. Confirm that jars have sealed, then store properly.

YIELD: 4 HALF-PINT (8-OUNCE, OR 236 ML) JARS

CUSTOMIZE IT!

If you're looking for something new, why not substitute some different fruits? In place of or in combination with the cherry and peach in this recipe, use pear, apricot, mango, fig, or sweet plum—or use a combination of any of these fruits.

ALL-FRUIT ORANGE JAM

If you're a fan of oranges, and you enjoy jam with breakfast daily, why not give this jam a try? Because it has no added white sugar, and is sweetened only with orange juice concentrate, it's a perfect option for everyday morning meals. Make it with the sweetest, freshest oranges you can find, as the taste of the fruit really shines through. Kids especially enjoy this jam, as it's kind of like getting to have an extra glass of orange juice with breakfast!

8 medium-size oranges

½ cup (120 ml) water

3 tablespoons (45 ml) lemon juice

3 teaspoons (15 ml) calcium water*

1½ cups (355 ml) unsweetened orange juice concentrate

5 teaspoons (15 g) Pomona's pectin powder

For information on how to prepare calcium water, refer to page 22.

1. If you are new to canning, or need a refresher, refer to chapter 1 (pages 12–41) for step-by-step guidance and additional information on how to safely can your jam. Once ready, proceed as follows.

2. Prepare your jars, lids, and bands; heat up your canner; and sterilize your jars.

3. Peel the oranges, and discard the peels. Remove and discard the seeds, the excess white pith, and the especially fibrous parts of the membrane from the flesh of all the oranges. Finely chop the flesh of the oranges.

4. In a large saucepan, combine chopped oranges and the ½ cup (120 ml) of water. Bring mixture to a boil over high heat. Reduce heat and simmer, covered, for 10 minutes, stirring occasionally. Remove from heat.

5. Measure out 4½ cups (1 L) of the cooked fruit (saving any remaining fruit for another use), and return the measured quantity to the saucepan. Add lemon juice and calcium water and mix well.

6. In a separate pan, bring orange juice concentrate to a boil. Pour hot juice concentrate in a blender or food processor, and then add pectin powder. Vent the lid and blend for 1 to 2 minutes, stopping to scrape down sides with a rubber spatula as needed, until pectin powder is thoroughly dissolved. Set aside.

7. Bring fruit mixture back to a full boil over high heat. Slowly add pectin–juice concentrate mixture, stirring constantly. Continue to cook and stir jam for 1 minute as the jam comes back up to a boil. Once the jam returns to a full boil, remove it from the heat.

8. **Can Your Jam:** Remove jars from canner and ladle jam into hot jars, leaving ¼ inch (6 mm) of headspace. Remove trapped air bubbles, wipe rims with a damp cloth, put on lids and screw bands, and tighten to fingertip tight. Lower filled jars into canner, ensuring jars are not touching each other and are covered with at least 1 to 2 inches (2.5 to 5 cm) of water. Place lid on canner, return to a rolling boil, and process for 10 minutes (adjusting for altitude if necessary). Turn off heat and allow canner to sit untouched for 5 minutes, then remove jars and allow to cool undisturbed for 12 to 24 hours. Confirm that jars have sealed, then store properly.

YIELD: 5 TO 6 HALF-PINT (8-OUNCE, OR 236 ML) JARS

BLUBARB JAM

The combination of blueberries and rhubarb is less common than the typical strawberry-rhubarb pairing, but it really shouldn't be—this lovely, deep blue jam is a delicious, tangy treat. This recipe was adapted from one by jam-maker Kirsten Jennings, who first tried it at a local restaurant and liked it so much that she figured out how to make it at home herself.

1 pound (455 g) blueberries*

1 pound (455 g) trimmed rhubarb stalks*

½ cup (120 ml) water

¼ cup (60 ml) lemon juice

2 teaspoons (10 ml) calcium water**

1¼ cups (250 g) sugar

2½ teaspoons (7.5 g) Pomona's pectin powder

*Not sure how much fruit to purchase? See "Measuring Up!" on page 26.

**For information on how to prepare calcium water, refer to page 22.

FROZEN EASE!

You can substitute frozen berries for the fresh, and if you don't have a lot of time, this is a good option. Simply defrost the berries, and then mash them as the recipe calls for. After defrosting, the berries will be in a lot of juice, but don't drain them—simply incorporate all of the juice into the mashed berries.

1. If you are new to canning, or need a refresher, refer to chapter 1 (pages 12–41) for step-by-step guidance and additional information on how to safely can your jam. Once ready, proceed as follows.
2. Prepare your jars, lids, and bands; heat up your canner; and sterilize your jars.
3. Rinse blueberries, remove stems, and mash in a large bowl. Set aside.
4. Rinse rhubarb, slice stalks lengthwise into thin strips, and then dice. Combine diced rhubarb in a saucepan with the ½ cup (120 ml) of water. Bring to a boil over high heat, reduce heat, and then simmer, covered, for 5 minutes, or until rhubarb is soft, stirring occasionally. Remove from heat and mash rhubarb.
5. Measure out 2 cups (473 ml) of the mashed blueberries and 2 cups (473 ml) of the mashed rhubarb (saving any extra for another use), and combine the measured quantities in a saucepan. Add lemon juice and the calcium water, and mix well.
6. In a separate bowl, combine sugar and pectin powder. Mix thoroughly and set aside.
7. Bring fruit mixture to a full boil over high heat. Slowly add pectin-sugar mixture, stirring constantly. Continue to stir vigorously for 1 to 2 minutes to dissolve pectin while the jam comes back up to a boil. Once the jam returns to a full boil, remove it from the heat.
8. **Can Your Jam:** Remove jars from canner and ladle jam into hot jars, leaving ¼ inch (6 mm) of headspace. Remove trapped air bubbles, wipe rims with a damp cloth, put on lids and screw bands, and tighten to fingertip tight. Lower filled jars into canner, ensuring jars are not touching each other and are covered with at least 1 to 2 inches (2.5 to 5 cm) of water. Place lid on canner, return to a rolling boil, and process for 10 minutes (adjusting for altitude if necessary). Turn off heat and allow canner to sit untouched for 5 minutes, then remove jars and allow to cool undisturbed for 12 to 24 hours. Confirm that jars have sealed, then store properly.

YIELD: 4 TO 5 HALF-PINT (8-OUNCE, OR 236 ML) JARS

GINGER-VANILLA-RHUBARB JAM

In this jam, adapted from a recipe by jam-maker Kirsten Jennings, the zesty bite of ginger beautifully complements the tang of rhubarb, and the vanilla adds an unexpected note of smoothness. Use deep red rhubarb stalks if you can find them—as Kirsten says, it will give your jam a gorgeous, rich red color.

2 pounds (907 g) trimmed rhubarb stalks*

2 teaspoons (5.4 g) peeled, finely grated ginger root (for more information, see "Grate That Ginger!" on page 125)

1 cup (235 ml) water

1 vanilla bean

¼ cup (60 ml) lemon juice

2 teaspoons (10 ml) calcium water**

1¼ cups (250 g) sugar

3 teaspoons (9 g) Pomona's pectin powder

*Not sure how much fruit to purchase? See "Measuring Up!" on page 26.

**For information on how to prepare calcium water, refer to page 22.

VERY VANILLA

Vanilla beans are long, slender, dark brown pods that grow on orchid vines in tropical regions. The tiny seeds inside the bean pod are what's generally used in cooking and baking. Mexican, Tahitian, and Madagascar Bourbon vanilla beans are the commercially available varieties, and they are all quite pricey (but so worth it!). Look for beans that are plump, and feel slightly oily. They can be found in some grocery stores and many specialty food shops.

1. If you are new to canning, or need a refresher, refer to chapter 1 (pages 12–41) for step-by-step guidance and additional information on how to safely can your jam. Once ready, proceed as follows.
2. Prepare your jars, lids, and bands; heat up your canner; and sterilize your jars.
3. Rinse rhubarb, slice stalks lengthwise into thin strips, and then dice. Combine diced rhubarb in a saucepan with grated ginger and the 1 cup (235 ml) of water.
4. Using a paring knife, slice the vanilla bean in half lengthwise and scrape out the seeds. Add the vanilla seeds and the bean pod itself to the rhubarb.
5. Bring rhubarb to a boil over high heat, reduce heat, and then simmer, covered, for 5 minutes, or until rhubarb is soft, stirring occasionally. Remove from heat and then mash the rhubarb.
6. Measure out 4 cups (946 ml) of the cooked rhubarb-ginger mixture (saving any extra for another use), and return the measured quantity to the saucepan. Add lemon juice and calcium water, and mix well.
7. In a separate bowl, combine sugar and pectin powder. Mix thoroughly and set aside.
8. Bring rhubarb mixture to a full boil over high heat. Slowly add pectin-sugar mixture, stirring constantly. Continue to stir vigorously for 1 to 2 minutes to dissolve pectin while the jam comes back up to a boil. Once the jam returns to a full boil, remove it from the heat. Using tongs, carefully remove the vanilla bean pod and discard.
9. **Can Your Jam:** Remove jars from canner and ladle jam into hot jars, leaving ¼ inch (6 mm) of headspace. Remove trapped air bubbles, wipe rims with a damp cloth, put on lids and screw bands, and tighten to fingertip tight. Lower filled jars into canner, ensuring jars are not touching each other and are covered with at least 1 to 2 inches (2.5 to 5 cm) of water. Place lid on canner, return to a rolling boil, and process for 10 minutes (adjusting for altitude if necessary). Turn off heat and allow canner to sit untouched for 5 minutes, then remove jars and allow to cool undisturbed for 12 to 24 hours. Confirm that jars have sealed, then store properly.

YIELD: 4 TO 5 HALF-PINT (8-OUNCE, OR 236 ML) JARS

MAPLE-VANILLA-PEACH JAM

If I were to eat any jam by the spoonful (which I admit to doing, on occasion), this would be the one. I also love a big dollop of it on top of vanilla ice cream. It's great in baked goods, too—as a filling for cookie bars, or even turnovers. The deep intensity of maple and vanilla, combined with the lusciousness of fresh peaches, is just heavenly.

3¼ pounds (1.5 kg) fully ripe peaches*

1 vanilla bean

¼ cup (60 ml) lemon juice

4 teaspoons (20 ml) calcium water**

¾ cup (175 ml) pure maple syrup (for more information, see "Go for the Real Thing!" on page 182)

3 teaspoons (9 g) Pomona's pectin powder

*Not sure how much fruit to purchase? See "Measuring Up!" on page 26.

**For information on how to prepare calcium water, refer to page 22.

1. If you are new to canning, or need a refresher, refer to chapter 1 (pages 12–41) for step-by-step guidance and additional information on how to safely can your jam. Once ready, proceed as follows.
2. Prepare your jars, lids, and bands; heat up your canner; and sterilize your jars.
3. Peel and remove pits from peaches, and then mash the peaches in a large bowl. (For more information, see "How to Skin a Peach" on page 58.)
4. Measure 4 cups (946 ml) of the mashed peaches (saving any extra for another use), and pour the measured amount into a saucepan. Using a paring knife, slice the vanilla bean in half lengthwise and scrape out the seeds. Add the vanilla seeds and the bean pod itself to the fruit, along with the lemon juice and calcium water. Mix well.
5. In a separate bowl, combine maple syrup and pectin powder. Mix thoroughly and set aside.
6. Bring fruit to a full boil over high heat. Slowly add pectin–maple syrup mixture, stirring constantly. Continue to stir vigorously for 1 to 2 minutes to dissolve pectin while the jam comes back up to a boil. Once the jam returns to a full boil, remove it from the heat. Using tongs, carefully remove the vanilla bean pod from the jam and discard.
7. **Can Your Jam:** Remove jars from canner and ladle jam into hot jars, leaving ¼ inch (6 mm) of headspace. Remove trapped air bubbles, wipe rims with a damp cloth, put on lids and screw bands, and tighten to fingertip tight. Lower filled jars into canner, ensuring jars are not touching each other and are covered with at least 1 to 2 inches (2.5 to 5 cm) of water. Place lid on canner, return to a rolling boil, and process for 10 minutes (adjusting for altitude if necessary). Turn off heat and allow canner to sit untouched for 5 minutes, then remove jars and allow to cool undisturbed for 12 to 24 hours. Confirm that jars have sealed, then store properly.

YIELD: 4 TO 5 HALF-PINT (8-OUNCE, OR 236 ML) JARS

PERFECT PEACHES!

This recipe requires mashed peaches, so be sure that your peaches are fully ripe and soft enough to mash. If they're not, however, simply place peeled, pitted, chopped peaches in a saucepan with ½ cup (120 ml) water. Simmer for 5 minutes to soften them, and then mash. (There is no need to drain the water after cooking—simply mash the peach mixture as is.)

HONEYED GINGER-PEACH JAM

The combination of ginger and peach is one of my favorites—the subtle heat of the ginger sets off the straight-ahead sweetness of fully ripe peaches just a bit, and the honey adds additional depth to this jam. Enjoy it with scones on a warm summer morning!

3¼ pounds (1.5 kg) fully ripe peaches*
(for more information, see "Perfect
Peaches!" on page 57)

2 teaspoons (5.4 g) peeled, finely
grated ginger root (for more
information, see "Grate That Ginger!"
on page 125)

¼ cup (60 ml) lemon juice

4 teaspoons (20 ml) calcium water**

½ cup (170 g) honey

3 teaspoons (9 g) Pomona's pectin
powder

*Not sure how much fruit to purchase?
See "Measuring Up!" on page 26.

**For information on how to prepare
calcium water, refer to page 22.

1. If you are new to canning, or need a refresher, refer to chapter 1 (pages 12–41) for step-by-step guidance and additional information on how to safely can your jam. Once ready, proceed as follows.
2. Prepare your jars, lids, and bands; heat up your canner; and sterilize your jars.
3. Peel and remove pits from peaches, and then mash the peaches in a large bowl.
4. Measure 4 cups (946 ml) of mashed peaches (saving any extra for another use), and combine the measured quantity in a saucepan with ginger, lemon juice, and calcium water. Mix well.
5. In a separate bowl, combine honey and pectin powder. Mix thoroughly and set aside.
6. Bring peach mixture to a full boil over high heat. Slowly add pectin-honey mixture, stirring constantly. Continue to stir vigorously for 1 to 2 minutes to dissolve pectin while the jam comes back up to a boil. Once the jam returns to a full boil, remove it from the heat.
7. **Can Your Jam:** Remove jars from canner and ladle jam into hot jars, leaving ¼ inch (6 mm) of headspace. Remove trapped air bubbles, wipe rims with a damp cloth, put on lids and screw bands, and tighten to fingertip tight. Lower filled jars into canner, ensuring jars are not touching each other and are covered with at least 1 to 2 inches (2.5 to 5 cm) of water. Place lid on canner, return to a rolling boil, and process for 10 minutes (adjusting for altitude if necessary). Turn off heat and allow canner to sit untouched for 5 minutes, then remove jars and allow to cool undisturbed for 12 to 24 hours. Confirm that jars have sealed, then store properly.

YIELD: 4 TO 5 HALF-PINT (8-OUNCE, OR 236 ML) JARS

HOW TO SKIN A PEACH

If you are dealing with a small quantity of fruit, slice off peach (or nectarine) skins with a paring knife (pitting and quartering the fruit first). However, if you're doubling the recipe and are working with a lot of fruit, you may want to blanch them to remove the skins instead. Simply drop peaches or nectarines one at a time into boiling water for about 30 to 60 seconds, then remove and immediately dunk in cold water. You should then be able to slip the skins right off.

HONEYED STRAWBERRY-RHUBARB JAM

In Maine at least, rhubarb is ready in early June, and the only other fruit in season at a somewhat similar time of year is strawberries, following just a little bit later in the month. So, it's no surprise that strawberries and rhubarb are a classic—not to mention delicious—flavor combination. The addition of honey makes this lovely, soft-set jam just a little bit different, perfect for swirling into yogurt or spooning over ice cream.

1 pound (455 g) strawberries*

1 pound (455 g) trimmed rhubarb stalks*

½ cup (120 ml) water

2 tablespoons (30 ml) lemon juice

2 teaspoons (10 ml) calcium water**

1¼ cups (425 g) honey

2½ teaspoons (7.5 g) Pomona's pectin powder

*Not sure how much fruit to purchase? See "Measuring Up!" on page 26.

**For information on how to prepare calcium water, refer to page 22.

1. If you are new to canning, or need a refresher, refer to chapter 1 (pages 12–41) for step-by-step guidance and additional information on how to safely can your jam. Once ready, proceed as follows.
2. Prepare your jars, lids, and bands; heat up your canner; and sterilize your jars.
3. Rinse strawberries, remove stems, and mash in a large bowl. Set aside.
4. Rinse rhubarb, slice stalks lengthwise into thin strips, and then dice. Combine diced rhubarb in a saucepan with the ½ cup (120 ml) of water. Bring to a boil over high heat, reduce heat, and then simmer, covered, for 5 minutes, or until rhubarb is soft, stirring occasionally. Remove from heat and mash rhubarb.
5. Measure 2 cups (473 ml) of the mashed strawberries and 2 cups (473 ml) of the mashed rhubarb (saving any extra for another use), and combine the measured quantities in a saucepan with lemon juice and calcium water. Mix well.
6. In a separate bowl, combine honey and pectin powder. Mix thoroughly and set aside.
7. Bring fruit mixture to a full boil over high heat. Slowly add the pectin-honey mixture, stirring constantly. Continue to stir vigorously for 1 to 2 minutes to dissolve pectin while the jam comes back up to a boil. Once the jam returns to a full boil, remove it from the heat.
8. **Can Your Jam:** Remove jars from canner and ladle jam into hot jars, leaving ¼ inch (6 mm) of headspace. Remove trapped air bubbles, wipe rims with a damp cloth, put on lids and screw bands, and tighten to fingertip tight. Lower filled jars into canner, ensuring jars are not touching each other and are covered with at least 1 to 2 inches (2.5 to 5 cm) of water. Place lid on canner, return to a rolling boil, and process for 10 minutes (adjusting for altitude if necessary). Turn off heat and allow canner to sit untouched for 5 minutes, then remove jars and allow to cool undisturbed for 12 to 24 hours. Confirm that jars have sealed, then store properly.

YIELD: 4 TO 5 HALF-PINT (8-OUNCE, OR 236 ML) JARS

FROZEN EASE!

You can substitute frozen berries for the fresh, and if you don't have a lot of time, this is a good option. Simply defrost the berries, and then mash them as the recipe calls for. After defrosting, the berries will be in a lot of juice, but don't drain them—simply incorporate all of the juice into the mashed berries.

MANGO-LIME JAM

The tang of lime beautifully balances the intense sweetness of mangoes in this easy-to-make, sweet-and-sour, golden-colored jam. It's delicious slathered on toast, of course, but for an unexpected treat, try it alongside grilled chicken and perhaps a spicy rice dish.

4 pounds (1.8 kg) fully ripe mangoes* (for more information, see "Do The Mango Mash!" on page 167)

½ cup (120 ml) lime juice

4 teaspoons (20 ml) calcium water**

1 cup (200 g) sugar

3 teaspoons (9 g) Pomona's pectin powder

*Not sure how much fruit to purchase? See "Measuring Up!" on page 26.

**For information on how to prepare calcium water, refer to page 22.

MANGO MADNESS!

Mangoes can be maddening if you don't know how to prepare them. To cut up a mango with ease, hold the mango upright, and, starting from the top, slice down along one of the flat sides of the mango, cutting close along the flat side of the pit, slicing off as much flesh as possible. Then repeat the process on the opposite flat side of the mango. Gently score the flesh of each of the sliced-off sides of the mango in a grid pattern, and then push the skins inside out and carefully slice the mango cubes off the skins. Also slice off and cut up any flesh remaining on the pit before discarding skins and pit.

1. If you are new to canning, or need a refresher, refer to chapter 1 (pages 12–41) for step-by-step guidance and additional information on how to safely can your jam. Once ready, proceed as follows.
2. Prepare your jars, lids, and bands; heat up your canner; and sterilize your jars.
3. Peel and pit mangoes, and then mash in a large bowl.
4. Measure 4 cups (946 ml) of mashed mango (saving any extra for another use), and combine the measured quantity in a saucepan with lime juice and calcium water. Mix well.
5. In a separate bowl, combine sugar and pectin powder. Mix thoroughly and set aside.
6. Bring mango mixture to a full boil over high heat. Slowly add pectin-sugar mixture, stirring constantly. Continue to stir vigorously for 1 to 2 minutes to dissolve pectin while the jam comes back up to a boil. Once the jam returns to a full boil, remove it from the heat.
7. **Can Your Jam:** Remove jars from canner and ladle jam into hot jars, leaving ¼ inch (6 mm) of headspace. Remove trapped air bubbles, wipe rims with a damp cloth, put on lids and screw bands, and tighten to fingertip tight. Lower filled jars into canner, ensuring jars are not touching each other and are covered with at least 1 to 2 inches (2.5 to 5 cm) of water. Place lid on canner, return to a rolling boil, and process for 10 minutes (adjusting for altitude if necessary). Turn off heat and allow canner to sit untouched for 5 minutes, then remove jars and allow to cool undisturbed for 12 to 24 hours. Confirm that jars have sealed, then store properly.

YIELD: 4 TO 5 HALF-PINT (8-OUNCE, OR 236 ML) JARS

STRAWBERRY-MANGO JAM

This delicious, pink jam is a perfect combination of the full-on, exotic sweetness of ripe mangoes, with the luscious, fragrant, slightly tart flavor of in-season, locally grown strawberries. I can't imagine a better jam to enjoy on muffins, outside, on a warm June morning.

1 pound (455 g) strawberries*

2 pounds (910 g) fully ripe mangoes*

2 tablespoons (30 ml) lemon juice

3 teaspoons (15 ml) calcium water**

1 cup (200 g) sugar

2½ teaspoons (7.5 g) Pomona's pectin powder

Not sure how much fruit to purchase? See "Measuring Up!" on page 26.

**For information on how to prepare calcium water, refer to page 22.*

1. If you are new to canning, or need a refresher, refer to chapter 1 (pages 12–41) for step-by-step guidance and additional information on how to safely can your jam. Once ready, proceed as follows.
2. Prepare your jars, lids, and bands; heat up your canner; and sterilize your jars.
3. Rinse strawberries, remove stems, and mash in a large bowl. Set aside.
4. Peel and pit mangoes, and then mash in a large bowl.
5. Measure 2 cups (473 ml) mashed mango and 2 cups (473 ml) mashed strawberries (saving any extra for another use), and combine the measured quantities in a saucepan with lemon juice and calcium water. Mix well.
6. In a separate bowl, combine sugar and pectin powder. Mix thoroughly and set aside.
7. Bring fruit mixture to a full boil over high heat. Slowly add pectin-sugar mixture, stirring constantly. Continue to stir vigorously for 1 to 2 minutes to dissolve pectin while the jam comes back up to a boil. Once the jam returns to a full boil, remove it from the heat.
8. **Can Your Jam:** Remove jars from canner and ladle jam into hot jars, leaving ¼ inch (6 mm) of headspace. Remove trapped air bubbles, wipe rims with a damp cloth, put on lids and screw bands, and tighten to fingertip tight. Lower filled jars into canner, ensuring jars are not touching each other and are covered with at least 1 to 2 inches (2.5 to 5 cm) of water. Place lid on canner, return to a rolling boil, and process for 10 minutes (adjusting for altitude if necessary). Turn off heat and allow canner to sit untouched for 5 minutes, then remove jars and allow to cool undisturbed for 12 to 24 hours. Confirm that jars have sealed, then store properly.

YIELD: 4 TO 5 HALF-PINT (8-OUNCE, OR 236 ML) JARS

APPLE-MAPLE JAM

Even though maple syrup is made in the spring, I tend to think of it as an autumn sort of flavor, and perhaps that's why I enjoy it so much paired with apples. This simple, homey, mildly spiced jam is delicious on toast, of course, but it also makes a great filling or topping for turnovers, croissants, mini-tarts, and other baked goods. For the best texture, use crisp, hard apples that will retain their shape when cooked—Granny Smiths are a good choice.

2 pounds (910 g) apples*

2 cups (473 ml) water

½ teaspoon (1.25 g) ground cinnamon

⅓ cup (75 ml) lemon juice

4 teaspoons (20 ml) calcium water**

½ cup (120 ml) maple syrup

3 teaspoons (9 g) Pomona's pectin powder

*Not sure how much fruit to purchase? See "Measuring Up!" on page 26.

**For information on how to prepare calcium water, refer to page 22.

1. If you are new to canning, or need a refresher, refer to chapter 1 (pages 12–41) for step-by-step guidance and additional information on how to safely can your jam. Once ready, proceed as follows.
2. Prepare your jars, lids, and bands; heat up your canner; and sterilize your jars.
3. Peel apples, remove stems and cores, and dice.
4. Combine diced apples in a saucepan with the 2 cups (473 ml) water. Bring to a boil over high heat, reduce heat, and then simmer, covered, for 5 to 10 minutes, or until apples are soft, stirring occasionally. Remove from heat.
5. Measure 4 cups (946 ml) of cooked apples (saving any extra for another use), and return the measured quantity to the saucepan. Add cinnamon, lemon juice, and calcium water, and mix well.
6. In a separate bowl, combine maple syrup and pectin powder. Mix thoroughly and set aside.
7. Bring apple mixture back to full boil over high heat. Slowly add pectin–maple syrup mixture, stirring constantly. Continue to stir vigorously for 1 to 2 minutes to dissolve pectin while the jam comes back up to a boil. Once the jam returns to a full boil, remove it from the heat.
8. **Can Your Jam:** Remove jars from canner and ladle jam into hot jars, leaving ¼ inch (6 mm) of headspace. Remove trapped air bubbles, wipe rims with a damp cloth, put on lids and screw bands, and tighten to fingertip tight. Lower filled jars into canner, ensuring jars are not touching each other and are covered with at least 1 to 2 inches (2.5 to 5 cm) of water. Place lid on canner, return to a rolling boil, and process for 10 minutes (adjusting for altitude if necessary). Turn off heat and allow canner to sit untouched for 5 minutes, then remove jars and allow to cool undisturbed for 12 to 24 hours. Confirm that jars have sealed, then store properly.

YIELD: 4 TO 5 HALF-PINT (8-OUNCE, OR 236 ML) JARS

HONEYED APRICOT-JALAPEÑO JAM

This deep orange jam is studded with pieces of sweet red pepper and spicy green jalapeños. An intriguing combination of sweet, sour, and hot, it can be a delicious kick start to your morning when slathered on a warm corn muffin with a bit of butter. It's equally wonderful, however, tucked into a grilled cheese sandwich. Remember, for canning safety, do not increase the quantity of any peppers in this recipe, and be sure to use bottled lime juice.

2½ pounds (1.1 kg) ripe apricots*

⅔ cup (80 g) seeded, finely diced red bell pepper

⅓ cup (45 g) seeded, finely chopped jalapeño pepper

⅔ cup (150 ml) lime juice, divided

4 teaspoons (20 ml) calcium water**

1 cup (340 g) honey

1 tablespoon (9 g) Pomona's pectin powder

*Not sure how much fruit to purchase? See "Measuring Up!" on page 26.

**For information on how to prepare calcium water, refer to page 22.

1. If you are new to canning, or need a refresher, refer to chapter 1 (pages 12–41) for step-by-step guidance and additional information on how to safely can your jam. Once ready, proceed as follows.
2. Prepare your jars, lids, and bands; heat up your canner; and sterilize your jars.
3. Rinse apricots, remove stems, and then slice in half or pull apart. Remove pits, and chop apricots into small pieces (For more information, see "To Peel or Not to Peel?" on page 76.)
4. Combine chopped apricots with bell peppers, jalapeño peppers, and 4 tablespoons (60 ml) of the lime juice in a saucepan. Cover, bring the mixture to a boil over high heat, and then reduce heat and simmer, still covered, for 15 minutes, stirring occasionally. Remove from heat, and then mash.
5. Measure 4 cups (946 ml) of the apricot mixture (saving any extra for another use), and combine the measured quantity in a saucepan with the remaining lime juice and the calcium water. Mix well.
6. In a separate bowl, combine honey and pectin powder. Mix thoroughly and set aside.
7. Bring fruit mixture to a full boil over high heat. Slowly add pectin-honey mixture, stirring constantly. Continue to stir vigorously for 1 to 2 minutes to dissolve pectin while the jam comes back up to a boil. Once the jam returns to a full boil, remove it from the heat.
8. **Can Your Jam:** Remove jars from canner and ladle jam into hot jars, leaving ¼ inch (6 mm) of headspace. Remove trapped air bubbles, wipe rims with a damp cloth, put on lids and screw bands, and tighten to fingertip tight. Lower filled jars into canner, ensuring jars are not touching each other and are covered with at least 1 to 2 inches (2.5 to 5 cm) of water. Place lid on canner, return to a rolling boil, and process for 10 minutes (adjusting for altitude if necessary). Turn off heat and allow canner to sit untouched for 5 minutes, then remove jars and allow to cool undisturbed for 12 to 24 hours. Confirm that jars have sealed, then store properly.

YIELD: 4 TO 5 HALF-PINT (8-OUNCE, OR 236 ML) JARS

HOT STUFF!

Hot peppers are, well, hot! Always wear gloves while chopping them to protect your hands from the heat, and be sure not to touch your face.

PEAR-GINGER JAM

I never tire of ginger's subtle, unique heat, and because of its warmth, it's a perfect flavor for fall. In my mind, the pear is truly the queen of fall fruit, so the combination of the two is a natural—and an absolutely delicious one at that. For a scrumptious treat, try this earthy, mildly spiced jam slathered on waffles on a cool autumn morning!

3¼ pounds (1.5 kg) fully ripe pears* (for more information, see "Perfect Pears!" below)

1 tablespoon (8 g) peeled, finely grated ginger root (for more information, see "Grate That Ginger!" on page 125)

¼ cup (60 ml) lemon juice

4 teaspoons (20 ml) calcium water**

1¼ cups (250 g) sugar

3 teaspoons (9 g) Pomona's pectin powder

*Not sure how much fruit to purchase? See "Measuring Up!" on page 26.

**For information on how to prepare calcium water, refer to page 22.

1. If you are new to canning, or need a refresher, refer to chapter 1 (pages 12–41) for step-by-step guidance and additional information on how to safely can your jam. Once ready, proceed as follows.
2. Prepare your jars, lids, and bands; heat up your canner; and sterilize your jars.
3. Peel and core pears, and then mash pears in a large bowl.
4. Measure 4 cups (946 ml) of mashed pear (saving any extra for another use), and combine the measured quantity in a saucepan with ginger, lemon juice, and calcium water. Mix well.
5. In a separate bowl, combine sugar and pectin powder. Mix thoroughly and set aside.
6. Bring fruit mixture to a full boil over high heat. Slowly add pectin-sugar mixture, stirring constantly. Continue to stir vigorously for 1 to 2 minutes to dissolve pectin while the jam returns to a boil. Once the jam returns to a full boil, remove it from the heat.
7. **Can Your Jam:** Remove jars from canner and ladle jam into hot jars, leaving ¼ inch (6 mm) of headspace. Remove trapped air bubbles, wipe rims with a damp cloth, put on lids and screw bands, and tighten to fingertip tight. Lower filled jars into canner, ensuring jars are not touching each other and are covered with at least 1 to 2 inches (2.5 to 5 cm) of water. Place lid on canner, return to a rolling boil, and process for 10 minutes (adjusting for altitude if necessary). Turn off heat and allow canner to sit untouched for 5 minutes, then remove jars and allow to cool undisturbed for 12 to 24 hours. Confirm that jars have sealed, then store properly.

YIELD: 4 TO 5 HALF-PINT (8-OUNCE, OR 236 ML) JARS

PERFECT PEARS!

This recipe requires mashed pears, so be sure that your pears are fully ripe and soft enough to mash. If they're not, however, simply place peeled, cored, chopped pears in a saucepan with ½ cup (120 ml) water. Simmer for 5 minutes to soften them, and then mash.(There is no need to drain the water after cooking—simply mash the pear mixture as is.)

STRAWBERRY-PINEAPPLE JAM with HONEY

If you love strawberry jam but are looking for something just a little bit different, give this delightful jam a try. Pineapple adds a little bit of tropical flair, and honey adds an earthy twist. Canned pineapple makes this jam quick to make, and because the pineapple is so naturally sweet, very little extra sweetener is necessary, so the flavors of both fruits really shine through.

1 pound (455 g) strawberries*

1 can (20 ounces, or 560 g) crushed, unsweetened pineapple in its own juice

2 teaspoons (10 ml) calcium water**

⅓ cup (115 g) honey

2 teaspoons (6 g) Pomona's pectin powder

Not sure how much fruit to purchase? See "Measuring Up!" on page 26.

**For information on how to prepare calcium water, refer to page 22.*

1. If you are new to canning, or need a refresher, refer to chapter 1 (pages 12–41) for step-by-step guidance and additional information on how to safely can your jam. Once ready, proceed as follows.
2. Prepare your jars, lids, and bands; heat up your canner; and sterilize your jars.
3. Rinse strawberries, remove stems, and mash in a large bowl. Add crushed pineapple (do not drain), and mix well to combine.
4. Measure 4 cups (946 ml) of the strawberry-pineapple mixture (saving any extra for another use), and combine the measured quantity in a saucepan with calcium water. Mix well.
5. In a separate bowl, combine honey and pectin powder. Mix thoroughly and set aside.
6. Bring strawberry-pineapple mixture to a full boil over high heat. Slowly add pectin-honey mixture, stirring constantly. Continue to stir vigorously for 1 to 2 minutes to dissolve pectin while the jam returns to a boil. Once the jam returns to a full boil, remove it from the heat.
7. **Can Your Jam:** Remove jars from canner and ladle jam into hot jars, leaving ¼ inch (6 mm) of headspace. Remove trapped air bubbles, wipe rims with a damp cloth, put on lids and screw bands, and tighten to fingertip tight. Lower filled jars into canner, ensuring jars are not touching each other and are covered with at least 1 to 2 inches (2.5 to 5 cm) of water. Place lid on canner, return to a rolling boil, and process for 10 minutes (adjusting for altitude if necessary). Turn off heat and allow canner to sit untouched for 5 minutes, then remove jars and allow to cool undisturbed for 12 to 24 hours. Confirm that jars have sealed, then store properly.

YIELD: 4 TO 5 HALF-PINT (8-OUNCE, OR 236 ML) JARS

SWEET CHERRY JAM

Adapted from a recipe by jam-maker Sally Gecks, this delightful, deep-red jam is a great option for cherry lovers who are keeping an eye on their sugar intake. It also makes a great on-the-go breakfast by layering it in a jar with some plain yogurt and granola. Be sure to use sweet cherries for this recipe—widely available Bing cherries are a great option. Unsweetened black cherry juice, sold in bottles, is available at most natural food stores.

2 pounds (910 g) sweet cherries*

1 cup (235 ml) unsweetened black cherry juice

¼ cup (60 ml) lemon juice

4 teaspoons (20 ml) calcium water**

⅓ cup (73 g) sugar

3 teaspoons (9 g) Pomona's pectin powder

*Not sure how much fruit to purchase? See "Measuring Up!" on page 26.

**For information on how to prepare calcium water, refer to page 22.

PAINLESS PITTING

Pitting cherries is really not hard, and it doesn't take that long. A cherry pitter (a hand-held device that removes pits) is handy—and if you have one already, great—but it's certainly not necessary. All of the recipes in this book call for either cherry halves or chopped cherries, so simply slice cherries in half vertically with a paring knife and pick out the pit with your fingers. It's as easy as that!

1. If you are new to canning, or need a refresher, refer to chapter 1 (pages 12–41) for step-by-step guidance and additional information on how to safely can your jam. Once ready, proceed as follows.
2. Prepare your jars, lids, and bands; heat up your canner; and sterilize your jars.
3. Rinse cherries, remove stems, slice in half, remove pits, and then chop the cherries—by hand with a chef's knife, or with a food processor.
4. Combine chopped cherries and black cherry juice and mix well. Measure 4 cups (946 ml) of the cherry mixture (saving any extra for another use), and combine the measured quantity in a saucepan with lemon juice and calcium water. Mix well.
5. In a separate bowl, combine sugar and pectin powder. Mix thoroughly and set aside.
6. Bring fruit to a full boil over high heat. Slowly add sugar-pectin mixture, stirring constantly. Continue to stir vigorously for 1 to 2 minutes to dissolve pectin while the jam comes back up to a boil. Once the jam returns to a full boil, remove it from the heat.
7. **Can Your Jam:** Remove jars from canner and ladle jam into hot jars, leaving ¼ inch (6 mm) of headspace. Remove trapped air bubbles, wipe rims with a damp cloth, put on lids and screw bands, and tighten to fingertip tight. Lower filled jars into canner, ensuring jars are not touching each other and are covered with at least 1 to 2 inches (2.5 to 5 cm) of water. Place lid on canner, return to a rolling boil, and process for 10 minutes (adjusting for altitude if necessary). Turn off heat and allow canner to sit untouched for 5 minutes, then remove jars and allow to cool undisturbed for 12 to 24 hours. Confirm that jars have sealed, then store properly.

YIELD: 4 TO 5 HALF-PINT (8-OUNCE, OR 236 ML) JARS

PINEAPPLE-APRICOT JAM

Adapted from a recipe by jam-maker Carol Sue Piros, this golden-orange jam is a tasty, bright, and sunny addition to any breakfast table, and it's wonderful served atop cottage cheese. It's quick to make, too, as it includes canned pineapple rather than fresh.

1 pound (455 g) fully ripe apricots*
(For more information, see "Apricot Angst" on page 46.)

1 can (20 ounces, or 560 g) crushed, unsweetened pineapple in its own juice

¼ cup (60 ml) lemon juice

3 teaspoons (15 ml) calcium water**

1 cup (200 g) sugar

2½ teaspoons (7.5 g) Pomona's pectin powder

*Not sure how much fruit to purchase? See "Measuring Up!" on page 26.

**For information on how to prepare calcium water, refer to page 22.

1. If you are new to canning, or need a refresher, refer to chapter 1 (pages 12–41) for step-by-step guidance and additional information on how to safely can your jam. Once ready, proceed as follows.
2. Prepare your jars, lids, and bands; heat up your canner; and sterilize your jars.
3. Rinse apricots, remove stems, and then slice in half or pull apart. Remove pits, chop apricots into small pieces, and mash in a large bowl.
4. Add the can of crushed pineapple (do *not* drain) to the mashed apricots and mix well. Measure 4 cups (946 ml) of the fruit mixture (saving any extra for another use), and combine the measured quantity in a saucepan with lemon juice and calcium water. Mix well.
5. In a separate bowl, combine sugar and pectin powder. Mix thoroughly and set aside.
6. Bring fruit to a full boil over high heat. Slowly add pectin-sugar mixture, stirring constantly. Continue to stir vigorously for 1 to 2 minutes to dissolve pectin while the jam comes back up to a boil. Once the jam returns to a full boil, remove it from the heat.
7. **Can Your Jam:** Remove jars from canner and ladle jam into hot jars, leaving ¼ inch (6 mm) of headspace. Remove trapped air bubbles, wipe rims with a damp cloth, put on lids and screw bands, and tighten to fingertip tight. Lower filled jars into canner, ensuring jars are not touching each other and are covered with at least 1 to 2 inches (2.5 to 5 cm) of water. Place lid on canner, return to a rolling boil, and process for 10 minutes (adjusting for altitude if necessary). Turn off heat and allow canner to sit untouched for 5 minutes, then remove jars and allow to cool undisturbed for 12 to 24 hours. Confirm that jars have sealed, then store properly.

YIELD: 4 TO 5 HALF-PINT (8-OUNCE, OR 236 ML) JARS

CUSTOMIZE IT!

This recipe calls for slightly more pineapple than apricot, but if you prefer more apricot, feel free to vary the fruit ratio, bumping up the quantity of apricots and reducing the amount of pineapple—just remember to keep the total quantity of mixed fruit at 4 cups (946 ml).

HOLIDAY SPICED-PLUM JAM

Despite its name, plum pudding—the classic British dessert—is not made with plums. I've always thought plums would be good in it, though, which is how I got the idea for this wintery holiday jam. It's perfect atop thumbprint cookies (pictured here on plain thumbprints, alongside an almond version topped with our Simple Classic: Raspberry Preserves, page 109).

2 pounds (910 g) ripe, sweet plums*

1 cup (145 g) raisins, finely chopped

¼ cup (60 ml) orange juice

¾ cup (175 ml) brandy

½ teaspoon (1.25 g) ground cinnamon

½ teaspoon (1.25 g) ground ginger

½ teaspoon (1.5 g) ground cloves

¼ cup (60 ml) lemon juice

4 teaspoons (20 ml) calcium water**

1¼ cups (181.3 g) unpacked brown sugar

3 teaspoons (9 g) Pomona's pectin powder

*Not sure how much fruit to purchase? See "Measuring Up!" on page 26.

**For information on how to prepare calcium water, refer to page 22.

CUSTOMIZE IT!

If you're looking for something a little different, why not try honey instead of sugar in this recipe? In place of the sugar, use ½ to 1 cup (170 to 340 g) of honey.

1. If you are new to canning, or need a refresher, refer to chapter 1 (pages 12–41) for step-by-step guidance and additional information on how to safely can your jam. Once ready, proceed as follows.
2. Prepare your jars, lids, and bands; heat up your canner; and sterilize your jars.
3. Rinse plums, remove stems, and slice in half. Remove pits, and then chop the plums. (For more information, see "To Peel or Not to Peel?" on page 76.)
4. Combine chopped plums, finely chopped raisins, orange juice, brandy, cinnamon, ginger, and cloves in a saucepan. Bring fruit mixture to a boil over high heat, reduce heat, and then simmer, covered, for 10 to 15 minutes, or until fruit is soft, stirring occasionally. Remove from heat and mash the plum mixture.
5. Measure 4 cups (946 ml) of the mashed plum mixture (saving any extra for another use), and return measured quantity to the saucepan. Add lemon juice and calcium water and mix well.
6. In a separate bowl, combine brown sugar and pectin powder. Mix thoroughly and set aside.
7. Bring fruit to a full boil over high heat. Slowly add pectin-sugar mixture, stirring constantly. Continue to stir vigorously for 1 to 2 minutes to dissolve pectin while the jam comes back up to a boil. Once the jam returns to a full boil, remove it from the heat.
8. **Can Your Jam:** Remove jars from canner and ladle jam into hot jars, leaving ¼ inch (6 mm) of headspace. Remove trapped air bubbles, wipe rims with a damp cloth, put on lids and screw bands, and tighten to fingertip tight. Lower filled jars into canner, ensuring jars are not touching each other and are covered with at least 1 to 2 inches (2.5 to 5 cm) of water. Place lid on canner, return to a rolling boil, and process for 10 minutes (adjusting for altitude if necessary). Turn off heat and allow canner to sit untouched for 5 minutes, then remove jars and allow to cool undisturbed for 12 to 24 hours. Confirm that jars have sealed, then store properly.

YIELD: 4 TO 5 HALF-PINT (8-OUNCE, OR 236 ML) JARS

BASIL-MINT-PLUM JAM

Adapted from a recipe by jam maker Kirsten Jennings, this lovely, deep-purple jam is infused with the refreshing and unexpected flavor combination of mint and basil. As Kirsten says, "One summer we added fresh herbs from our garden to a plate of sliced plums—and the idea for this jam was born." If you can't find Thai basil, the more commonly available Genovese basil is a good substitute.

2½ pounds (1.1 kg) ripe, sweet plums*

¼ cup (60 ml) water

2 teaspoons (2.75 g) finely chopped fresh mint

2 teaspoons (5 g) finely chopped fresh Thai basil

⅓ cup (75 ml) lime juice

4 teaspoons (20 ml) calcium water**

1 cup (200 g) sugar

3 teaspoons (9 g) Pomona's pectin powder

*Not sure how much fruit to purchase? See "Measuring Up!" on page 26.

**For information on how to prepare calcium water, refer to page 22.

1. If you are new to canning, or need a refresher, refer to chapter 1 (pages 12–41) for step-by-step guidance and additional information on how to safely can your jam. Once ready, proceed as follows.
2. Prepare your jars, lids, and bands; heat up your canner; and sterilize your jars.
3. Rinse plums, remove stems, and slice in half. Remove pits, and then chop the plums.
4. Combine plums in a saucepan with the ¼ cup (60 ml) water and finely chopped mint and basil. Bring fruit mixture to a boil over high heat, reduce heat, and then simmer, covered, for 5 to 10 minutes, or until fruit is soft, stirring occasionally. Remove from heat, and then mash plums.
5. Measure 4 cups (946 ml) of the mashed plum mixture (saving any extra for another use), and combine measured quantity in a saucepan with lime juice and calcium water. Mix well.
6. In a separate bowl, combine sugar and pectin powder. Mix thoroughly and set aside.
7. Bring fruit to a full boil over high heat. Slowly add pectin-sugar mixture, stirring constantly. Continue to stir vigorously for 1 to 2 minutes to dissolve pectin while the jam comes back up to a boil. Once the jam returns to a full boil, remove it from the heat.
8. **Can Your Jam:** Remove jars from canner and ladle jam into hot jars, leaving ¼ inch (6 mm) of headspace. Remove trapped air bubbles, wipe rims with a damp cloth, put on lids and screw bands, and tighten to fingertip tight. Lower filled jars into canner, ensuring jars are not touching each other and are covered with at least 1 to 2 inches (2.5 to 5 cm) of water. Place lid on canner, return to a rolling boil, and process for 10 minutes (adjusting for altitude if necessary). Turn off heat and allow canner to sit untouched for 5 minutes, then remove jars and allow to cool undisturbed for 12 to 24 hours. Confirm that jars have sealed, then store properly.

YIELD: 4 TO 5 HALF-PINT (8-OUNCE, OR 236 ML) JARS

TO PEEL OR NOT TO PEEL?

*When it comes to plums and apricots, my answer to this question is always **not to peel**. Unlike peaches, plum and apricot skins take a bit of effort to remove. Fortunately, though, their skins are so delicate they seem to disappear when cooked, so they are almost imperceptible. And, if you slice the fruit into smaller pieces before mashing, the skins are even less noticeable. Some folks do choose to skin plums and apricots, but I prefer to leave the skins on.*

KIWI-LIME JAM

If you're a fan of sweet and sour, you'll love this green-hued jam with a kick of lime—it's a perfect combination of tart and sweet. The tiny black seeds of the kiwi also make this jam distinctive, providing just a bit of texture and crunch with each spoonful.

2¾ pounds (1.2 kg) ripe kiwis*

1 lime

2 teaspoons (10 ml) calcium water**

1¼ cups (250 g) sugar

2 teaspoons (6 g) Pomona's pectin powder

*Not sure how much fruit to purchase? See "Measuring Up!" on page 26.

**For information on how to prepare calcium water, refer to page 22.

1. If you are new to canning, or need a refresher, refer to chapter 1 (pages 12–41) for step-by-step guidance and additional information on how to safely can your jam. Once ready, proceed as follows.
2. Prepare your jars, lids, and bands; heat up your canner; and sterilize your jars.
3. Slice kiwis in half. Using a small spoon, scoop the fruit out of the skin and discard the peels. Mash the fruit by hand (don't use a food processor) in a large bowl.
4. Wash the lime thoroughly. Using a zester or a very fine grater, grate the exterior peel of the lime (avoiding the white interior of the peel) until you have accumulated ½ teaspoon of lime zest. Set zest aside. Slice lime in half and squeeze out the juice. Set the juice aside, and discard seeds and remaining peel.
5. Measure 4 cups (946 ml) of mashed kiwis (saving any extra for another use), and combine the measured quantity in a saucepan with lime zest, reserved lime juice, and calcium water. Mix well.
6. In a separate bowl, combine sugar and pectin powder. Mix thoroughly and set aside.
7. Bring kiwi mixture to a full boil over high heat. Slowly add pectin-sugar mixture, stirring constantly. Continue to stir vigorously for 1 to 2 minutes to dissolve pectin while the jam comes back up to a boil. Once the jam returns to a full boil, remove it from the heat.
8. **Can Your Jam:** Remove jars from canner and ladle jam into hot jars, leaving ¼ inch (6 mm) of headspace. Remove trapped air bubbles, wipe rims with a damp cloth, put on lids and screw bands, and tighten to fingertip tight. Lower filled jars into canner, ensuring jars are not touching each other and are covered with at least 1 to 2 inches (2.5 to 5 cm) of water. Place lid on canner, return to a rolling boil, and process for 10 minutes (adjusting for altitude if necessary). Turn off heat and allow canner to sit untouched for 5 minutes, then remove jars and allow to cool undisturbed for 12 to 24 hours. Confirm that jars have sealed, then store properly.

YIELD: 4 TO 5 HALF-PINT (8-OUNCE, OR 236 ML) JARS

BALSAMIC-FIG JAM

In my mind, a fresh fig is truly one of the world's most exquisite fruits. They don't ship all that well, and their beauty and flavor is fleeting, so if you live where these beauties grow fresh, you are indeed lucky! The complex flavor and acidity of balsamic vinegar is an ideal counterpoint to the sweet intensity of figs in this thick, rich, deeply colored jam. Serve it on a small slice of baguette with a bit of fresh goat cheese for an amazing flavor treat.

2¼ pounds (1 kg) figs*

1 cup (235 ml) water

½ cup (120 ml) balsamic vinegar

¼ teaspoon (0.45 g) cayenne pepper

¼ cup (60 ml) lemon juice

4 teaspoons (20 ml) calcium water**

1½ cups (300 g) sugar

3 teaspoons (9 g) Pomona's pectin powder

*Not sure how much fruit to purchase? See "Measuring Up!" on page 26.

**For information on how to prepare calcium water, refer to page 22.

CUSTOMIZE IT!

If you prefer a less-processed sugar, such as turbinado (raw sugar), you can use that instead of regular white sugar. Just be sure to pulse it in a food processor a few times to make the granules fine enough that you'll be able to mix the pectin into the sugar effectively.

1. If you are new to canning, or need a refresher, refer to chapter 1 (pages 12–41) for step-by-step guidance and additional information on how to safely can your jam. Once ready, proceed as follows.
2. Prepare your jars, lids, and bands; heat up your canner; and sterilize your jars.
3. Rinse figs, remove stems, and finely chop.
4. Combine chopped figs in saucepan with the 1 cup (235 ml) water. Bring to a boil over high heat, reduce heat, and then simmer, covered, for 5 to 10 minutes, or until fruit is soft, stirring occasionally. Remove from heat and mash the figs.
5. Measure 4 cups (946 ml) of the mashed figs (saving any extra for another use), and return the measured quantity to the saucepan. Add balsamic vinegar, cayenne pepper, lemon juice, and calcium water and mix well.
6. In a separate bowl, combine sugar and pectin powder. Mix thoroughly and set aside.
7. Bring fig mixture back to a full boil over high heat. Slowly add pectin-sugar mixture, stirring constantly. Continue to stir vigorously for 1 to 2 minutes to dissolve pectin while the jam comes back up to a boil. Once the jam returns to a full boil, remove it from the heat.
8. **Can Your Jam:** Remove jars from canner and ladle jam into hot jars, leaving ¼ inch (6 mm) of headspace. Remove trapped air bubbles, wipe rims with a damp cloth, put on lids and screw bands, and tighten to fingertip tight. Lower filled jars into canner, ensuring jars are not touching each other and are covered with at least 1 to 2 inches (2.5 to 5 cm) of water. Place lid on canner, return to a rolling boil, and process for 10 minutes (adjusting for altitude if necessary). Turn off heat and allow canner to sit untouched for 5 minutes, then remove jars and allow to cool undisturbed for 12 to 24 hours. Confirm that jars have sealed, then store properly.

YIELD: 4 TO 5 HALF-PINT (8-OUNCE, OR 236 ML) JARS

Chapter 3

JELLIES

Jellies are quite distinct from other pectin-jelled goods. Most jelled goods consist primarily of fruit that has been jelled, whereas jellies are the jelled *juice* of the fruit—or, in some cases, an infused liquid. Occasionally, a jelly will have something suspended in it—small pieces of pepper in a hot pepper jelly, for example—but generally speaking, jellies are smooth. Jellies can be intensely fruity and full-bodied but, because they are made from juice or an infused liquid, harnessing the essence of an item, rather than the item itself, jellies can also be very refined. They lend themselves nicely to flavors derived from items you might not necessarily want to eat whole and that are perhaps a bit more subtle, such as flowers or herbs. There is quite a diverse selection of flavors that can be incorporated into jellies. I've tried to include a wide variety of flavors and flavor combinations in this chapter—as well as a few classics, of course.

SIMPLE CLASSIC: APPLE JELLY

Apple jelly is a fall favorite, and it's a great way to use up extra apples during apple season. Even slightly soft apples that may have been hanging around for a while will work well for this recipe, as long as they are in good condition otherwise. With your pantry stocked, you'll be able to enjoy the lovely taste of apples in this delicate, golden jelly throughout the winter months! This is an easy recipe to start with if you're new to jelly making.

4 pounds (1.8 kg) apples*

4 cups (946 ml) water

¼ cup (60 ml) lemon juice

4 teaspoons (20 ml) calcium water**

1 cup (200 g) sugar

4 teaspoons (12 g) Pomona's pectin powder

*Not sure how much fruit to purchase? See "Measuring Up!" on page 26.

**For information on how to prepare calcium water, refer to page 22.

1. If you are new to canning, or need a refresher, refer to chapter 1 (pages 12–41) for step-by-step guidance and additional information on how to safely can your jelly. Once ready, proceed as follows.

2. Peel and core apples (if desired; for more information, see "Pit and Peel … or Not?" on page 94), and then chop. Combine chopped apples in a saucepan with the 4 cups (946 ml) of water. Bring to a boil over high heat, reduce heat, and simmer, covered, for 7 to 15 minutes, or until fruit is soft, stirring occasionally. Remove from heat and mash apples.

3. Transfer mashed fruit to a damp jelly bag or layered cheesecloth, suspend over a bowl, and allow juice to drip until dripping stops— at least 2 hours. Discard fruit pulp or save for another use.

4. Prepare your jars, lids, and bands; heat up your canner; and sterilize your jars.

5. Measure out 4 cups (946 ml) of the fruit juice (if you're short on juice, see "Where's the Juice?" on page 85 for more information) and combine in a saucepan with lemon juice and calcium water.

6. In a separate bowl, combine sugar and pectin powder. Mix thoroughly and set aside.

7. Bring juice to a full boil over high heat, and then slowly add pectin-sugar mixture, stirring constantly. Continue to stir vigorously for 1 to 2 minutes to dissolve pectin while the jelly comes back up to a boil. Once the jelly returns to a full boil, remove it from the heat.

8. **Can Your Jelly:** Remove jars from canner and ladle hot jelly into hot jars, leaving ¼ inch (6 mm) of headspace. Remove trapped air bubbles, wipe rims with a damp cloth, put on lids and screw bands, and tighten to fingertip tight. Lower filled jars into canner, ensuring jars are not touching each other and are covered with at least 1 to 2 inches (2.5 to 5 cm) of water. Place lid on canner, return to a rolling boil, and process for 10 minutes (adjusting for altitude if necessary). Turn off heat and allow canner to sit untouched for 5 minutes, then remove jars and allow to cool undisturbed for 12 to 24 hours. Confirm that jars have sealed, then store properly.

YIELD: 4 TO 5 HALF-PINT (8-OUNCE, OR 236 ML) JARS

CUSTOMIZE IT!

If you're looking for something new, why not try honey instead of sugar? In place of the sugar in this recipe, use ½ to 1 cup (170 to 340 g) honey.

SIMPLE CLASSIC: GRAPE JELLY

Almost everyone knows the ubiquitous, store-bought grape jelly of PB&J fame, but if you haven't tried homemade grape jelly, you're in for a real treat. With much less sugar than most commercially made versions, the true essence and natural sweetness of the grape really shines through in this gorgeous, dark purple jelly. This is an easy recipe to start with if you're new to jelly making.

4 pounds (1.8 kg) sweet black or purple grapes*

½ cup (120 ml) water

¼ cup (60 ml) lemon juice

4 teaspoons (20 ml) calcium water**

1 cup (200 g) sugar

4 teaspoons (12 g) Pomona's pectin powder

*Not sure how much fruit to purchase? See "Measuring Up!" on page 26.

**For information on how to prepare calcium water, refer to page 22.

CUSTOMIZE IT!

If you're looking for something new, try spicing it up! At the same time that you add the calcium water, add up to 1 teaspoon (2.5 g) of ground ginger, cardamom, cloves, cinnamon, nutmeg, or allspice. Or, you can mix and match these spices—just be sure that the total spice quantity does not exceed 1 teaspoon (2.5 g).

1. If you are new to canning, or need a refresher, refer to chapter 1 (pages 12–41) for step-by-step guidance and additional information on how to safely can your jelly. Once ready, proceed as follows.
2. Rinse grapes, remove stems, and combine in a saucepan with the ½ cup (120 ml) water. Bring to a boil over high heat, reduce heat, and then simmer, covered, for 8 to 10 minutes, stirring occasionally. Remove from heat and mash grapes.
3. Transfer mashed fruit to a damp jelly bag or layered cheesecloth, suspend over a bowl, and allow juice to drip until dripping stops—at least 2 hours. Discard fruit pulp or save for another use.
4. Prepare your jars, lids, and bands; heat up your canner; and sterilize your jars.
5. Carefully pour the juice out of its bowl, into another container, leaving the sediment in the bottom of the bowl. Discard the sediment. Measure 4 cups (946 ml) of the grape juice (if you're short on juice, see "Where's the Juice?" on page 85 for more information) and combine in a saucepan with lemon juice and calcium water. Mix well.
6. In a separate bowl, combine the sugar and the pectin powder. Mix thoroughly and set aside.
7. Bring the juice mixture to a full boil over high heat, and then slowly add the pectin-sugar mixture, stirring constantly. Continue to stir vigorously for 1 to 2 minutes to thoroughly dissolve pectin as the jelly comes back up to a boil. Once the jelly returns to a full boil, remove it from the heat.
8. **Can Your Jelly:** Remove jars from canner and ladle hot jelly into hot jars, leaving ¼ inch (6 mm) of headspace. Remove trapped air bubbles, wipe rims with a damp cloth, put on lids and screw bands, and tighten to fingertip tight. Lower filled jars into canner, ensuring jars are not touching each other and are covered with at least 1 to 2 inches (2.5 to 5 cm) of water. Place lid on canner, return to a rolling boil, and process for 10 minutes (adjusting for altitude if necessary). Turn off heat and allow canner to sit untouched for 5 minutes, then remove jars and allow to cool undisturbed for 12 to 24 hours. Confirm that jars have sealed, then store properly.

YIELD: 4 TO 5 HALF-PINT (8-OUNCE, OR 236 ML) JARS

SIMPLE CLASSIC: RASPBERRY JELLY

This dramatic, deep-red jelly is the essence of raspberry, intensified in a jar, and it's nothing short of amazing. It's also an easy recipe to start with if you're new to jelly making. Raspberries are precious, and jelly requires a lot of them, but if you're a true raspberry lover, the results will be worth it. Spread it on a piece of pound cake, layer it with some fresh fruit and whipped cream, or turn it into a trifle if you're really feeling fancy.

4 pounds (1.8 kg) raspberries*

⅓ cup (75 ml) water

4 teaspoons (20 ml) calcium water**

1½ cups (300 g) sugar

4 teaspoons (12 g) Pomona's pectin powder

*Not sure how much fruit to purchase? See "Measuring Up!" on page 26.

**For information on how to prepare calcium water, refer to page 22.

CUSTOMIZE IT!

If you're looking for something new, why not try different fruits? In place of or in combination with the raspberry in this recipe, use sour blackberry, currant, or strawberry—or use a combination of any of these fruits.

1. If you are new to canning, or need a refresher, refer to chapter 1 (pages 12–41) for step-by-step guidance and additional information on how to safely can your jelly. Once ready, proceed as follows.
2. Carefully pick through raspberries, removing stems and any damaged parts. Rinse raspberries only if necessary. Combine in a saucepan with the ⅓ cup (75 ml) water. Bring to a boil over high heat, reduce heat, and simmer, covered, for 1 to 2 minutes, stirring occasionally. Remove from heat and mash raspberries. (For more information and an alternative, see "Cook or Just Crush?" on page 98.)
3. Transfer mashed fruit to a damp jelly bag or layered cheesecloth, suspend over a bowl, and allow juice to drip until dripping stops—at least 2 hours. Discard fruit pulp or save for another use.
4. Prepare your jars, lids, and bands; heat up your canner; and sterilize your jars.
5. Measure 4 cups (946 ml) of the juice (if you're short on juice, see "Where's the Juice?" on page 85 for more information) and combine in a saucepan with calcium water.
6. In a separate bowl, combine sugar and pectin powder. Mix thoroughly and set aside.
7. Bring the juice mixture to a full boil over high heat, and then slowly add pectin-sugar mixture, stirring constantly. Continue to stir vigorously for 1 to 2 minutes to dissolve pectin while the jelly comes back up to a boil. Once the jelly returns to a full boil, remove it from the heat.
8. **Can Your Jelly:** Remove jars from canner and ladle hot jelly into hot jars, leaving ¼ inch (6 mm) of headspace. Remove trapped air bubbles, wipe rims with a damp cloth, put on lids and screw bands, and tighten to fingertip tight. Lower filled jars into canner, ensuring jars are not touching each other and are covered with at least 1 to 2 inches (2.5 to 5 cm) of water. Place lid on canner, return to a rolling boil, and process for 10 minutes (adjusting for altitude if necessary). Turn off heat and allow canner to sit untouched for 5 minutes, then remove jars and allow to cool undisturbed for 12 to 24 hours. Confirm that jars have sealed, then store properly.

YIELD: 4 TO 5 HALF-PINT (8-OUNCE, OR 236 ML) JARS

CRANAPPLE JELLY

Cranberry and apple is a classic flavor combination, and this brilliant, translucent, bright-red jelly highlights these two spectacular fall fruits. The tartness of the cranberries offsets the sweetness of the apples beautifully in this jelly, which makes a delicious—and gorgeous—addition to a warm bowl of steel-cut oats, or any autumn breakfast spread.

2¼ pounds (1 kg) apples*

1 bag (12 ounces, or 340 g) cranberries

3 cups (710 ml) water

¼ cup (60 ml) lemon juice

4 teaspoons (20 ml) calcium water**

1½ cups (300 g) sugar

4 teaspoons (12 g) Pomona's pectin powder

*Not sure how much fruit to purchase? See "Measuring Up!" on page 26.

**For information on how to prepare calcium water, refer to page 22.

WHERE'S THE JUICE?

What do you do if your jelly bag is done dripping, but you don't have enough juice? Slowly pour extra hot water—a very small amount at a time—onto the fruit pulp in the jelly bag, making sure it mixes with the fruit and drips out slowly, until you have the quantity of juice needed. Alternatively, you can dump the fruit pulp back in the pot with some extra water, cook for a few minutes, and then return the fruit to the jelly bag or cheesecloth to continue dripping until you have enough juice.

1. If you are new to canning, or need a refresher, refer to chapter 1 (pages 12–41) for step-by-step guidance and additional information on how to safely can your jelly. Once ready, proceed as follows.
2. Peel and core apples (if desired; for more information, see "Pit and Peel … Or Not?" on page 94), and then chop.
3. Rinse cranberries, and then combine in a saucepan with chopped apples and the 3 cups (710 ml) water. Bring to a boil over high heat, reduce heat, and simmer, covered, for 7 to 15 minutes, or until fruit is soft, stirring occasionally. Remove from heat and mash the fruit.
4. Transfer mashed fruit to a damp jelly bag or layered cheesecloth, suspend over a bowl, and allow juice to drip until dripping stops—at least 2 hours. Discard fruit pulp or save for another use.
5. Prepare your jars, lids, and bands; heat up your canner; and sterilize your jars.
6. Measure 4 cups (946 ml) of the fruit juice and combine in a saucepan with lemon juice and calcium water.
7. In a separate bowl, combine sugar and pectin powder. Mix thoroughly and set aside.
8. Bring fruit juice to a full boil over high heat, and then slowly add pectin-sugar mixture, stirring constantly. Continue to stir vigorously for 1 to 2 minutes to dissolve pectin while the jelly comes back up to a boil. Once the jelly returns to a full boil, remove it from the heat.
9. **Can Your Jelly:** Remove jars from canner and ladle hot jelly into hot jars, leaving ¼ inch (6 mm) of headspace. Remove trapped air bubbles, wipe rims with a damp cloth, put on lids and screw bands, and tighten to fingertip tight. Lower filled jars into canner, ensuring jars are not touching each other and are covered with at least 1 to 2 inches (2.5 to 5 cm) of water. Place lid on canner, return to a rolling boil, and process for 10 minutes (adjusting for altitude if necessary). Turn off heat and allow canner to sit untouched for 5 minutes, then remove jars and allow to cool undisturbed for 12 to 24 hours. Confirm that jars have sealed, then store properly.

YIELD: 4 TO 5 HALF-PINT (8-OUNCE, OR 236 ML) JARS

BLUEBERRY-VANILLA JELLY

A fresh vanilla bean adds a fragrant note of the exotic to just about any fruit, and this combination of blueberry and vanilla is one of my favorites. Try this luscious, deep-blue jelly slathered between the two layers of a cake for a spectacular, unexpected treat.

3½ pounds (1.6 kg) blueberries*

½ cup (120 ml) water

1 vanilla bean

¼ cup (60 ml) lemon juice

4 teaspoons (20 ml) calcium water**

1 cup (200 g) sugar

4 teaspoons (12 g) Pomona's pectin powder

Not sure how much fruit to purchase? See "Measuring Up!" on page 26.

**For information on how to prepare calcium water, refer to page 22.*

1. If you are new to canning, or need a refresher, refer to chapter 1 (pages 12–41) for step-by-step guidance and additional information on how to safely can your jelly. Once ready, proceed as follows.
2. Rinse blueberries, remove stems, and combine in a saucepan with the ½ cup (120 ml) of water. Bring to a boil over high heat, reduce heat, and simmer, covered, for 3 to 5 minutes, stirring frequently. Remove from heat and mash the blueberries.
3. Transfer mashed fruit to a damp jelly bag or layered cheesecloth, suspend over a bowl, and allow juice to drip until dripping stops—at least 2 hours. Discard fruit pulp or save for another use.
4. Prepare your jars, lids, and bands; heat up your canner; and sterilize your jars.
5. Measure 4 cups (946 ml) of the fruit juice (if you're short on juice, see "Where's the Juice?" on page 85 for more information) and pour into a saucepan. Using a paring knife, slice the vanilla bean in half lengthwise and scrape out the seeds. Add the vanilla seeds and the vanilla bean pod itself to the juice, along with the lemon juice and calcium water. Mix well.
6. In a separate bowl, combine sugar and pectin powder. Mix thoroughly and set aside.
7. Bring the blueberry mixture to a full boil over high heat, and then slowly add pectin-sugar mixture, stirring constantly. Continue to stir vigorously for 1 to 2 minutes to dissolve pectin while the jelly comes back up to a boil. Once the jelly returns to a full boil, remove it from the heat. Using tongs, carefully remove the vanilla bean pod and discard.
8. **Can Your Jelly:** Remove jars from canner and ladle hot jelly into hot jars, leaving ¼ inch (6 mm) of headspace. Remove trapped air bubbles, wipe rims with a damp cloth, put on lids and screw bands, and tighten to fingertip tight. Lower filled jars into canner, ensuring jars are not touching each other and are covered with at least 1 to 2 inches (2.5 to 5 cm) of water. Place lid on canner, return to a rolling boil, and process for 10 minutes (adjusting for altitude if necessary). Turn off heat and allow canner to sit untouched for 5 minutes, then remove jars and allow to cool undisturbed for 12 to 24 hours. Confirm that jars have sealed, then store properly.

YIELD: 4 TO 5 HALF-PINT (8-OUNCE, OR 236 ML) JARS

FROZEN EASE!

You can substitute frozen berries for the fresh, and if you don't have a lot of time, this is a good option. Simply cook the berries, and then mash them as the recipe calls for.

HONEYED PLUM-CARDAMOM JELLY

If you're lucky enough to have a plum tree (or have a friend who does!), and you have access to a good quantity of fresh plums in season, give this gorgeous, deep-purple jelly a try! Laced with the subtle, quietly complex flavor of cardamom, this jelly is a sophisticated accompaniment to scones at breakfast or afternoon tea.

4 pounds (1.8 kg) ripe, sweet plums*

1¼ cups (296 ml) water

1½ teaspoons (3.5 g) ground cardamom

¼ cup (60 ml) lemon juice

5 teaspoons (24.6 ml) calcium water**

1 cup (340 g) honey

5 teaspoons (15 g) Pomona's pectin powder

*Not sure how much fruit to purchase? See "Measuring Up!" on page 26.

**For information on how to prepare calcium water, refer to page 22.

1. If you are new to canning, or need a refresher, refer to chapter 1 (pages 12–41) for step-by-step guidance and additional information on how to safely can your jelly. Once ready, proceed as follows.
2. Rinse, remove pits, and quarter plums, and then combine in a saucepan with the 1¼ cups (296 ml) of water. Bring to a boil over high heat, reduce heat, and simmer, covered, for 7 to 15 minutes, or until fruit is soft, stirring occasionally. Remove from heat and mash plums.
3. Transfer mashed fruit to a damp jelly bag or layered cheesecloth, suspend over a bowl, and allow juice to drip until dripping stops—at least 2 hours. Discard fruit pulp or save for another use.
4. Prepare your jars, lids, and bands; heat up your canner; and sterilize your jars.
5. Measure 4 cups (946 ml) of the fruit juice (if you're short on juice, see "Where's the Juice?" on page 85 for more information) and combine in a saucepan with cardamom, lemon juice, and calcium water.
6. In a separate bowl, combine honey and pectin powder. Mix thoroughly and set aside.
7. Bring fruit juice to a full boil over high heat, and then slowly add pectin-honey mixture, stirring constantly. Continue to stir vigorously for 1 to 2 minutes to dissolve pectin while the jelly comes back up to a boil. Once the jelly returns to a full boil, remove it from the heat.
8. **Can Your Jelly:** Remove jars from canner and ladle hot jelly into hot jars, leaving ¼ inch (6 mm) of headspace. Remove trapped air bubbles, wipe rims with a damp cloth, put on lids and screw bands, and tighten to fingertip tight. Lower filled jars into canner, ensuring jars are not touching each other and are covered with at least 1 to 2 inches (2.5 to 5 cm) of water. Place lid on canner, return to a rolling boil, and process for 10 minutes (adjusting for altitude if necessary). Turn off heat and allow canner to sit untouched for 5 minutes, then remove jars and allow to cool undisturbed for 12 to 24 hours. Confirm that jars have sealed, then store properly.

YIELD: 4 TO 5 HALF-PINT (8-OUNCE, OR 236 ML) JARS

ORANGE-MANGO-MINT JELLY

My husband makes a delicious mango-mint sauce that inspired this jelly. The combination is refreshing and surprisingly addictive, and oranges add a touch of brightness to the mix. This jelly makes an excellent glaze for grilled tempeh or tofu and is a fabulous complement to most any Asian-inspired meal.

5½ pounds (2.5 kg) oranges*

2 pounds (910 g) ripe mangoes*

1 cup (46 g) coarsely chopped, firmly packed fresh mint leaves and stems

1½ cups (355 ml) water

¼ cup (60 ml) lime juice

4 teaspoons (20 ml) calcium water**

1 cup (200 g) sugar

4 teaspoons (12 g) Pomona's pectin powder

*Not sure how much fruit to purchase? See "Measuring Up!" on page 26.

**For information on how to prepare calcium water, refer to page 22.

DON'T SQUEEZE IT!

It's tempting to squeeze the cheesecloth or jelly bag to make the juice come out faster, but don't! If you do, you'll likely squeeze out small particles of fruit pulp in the process, which will make the juice cloudy. If you do find a little bit of pulp in your juice, do a quick pass through a fine mesh strainer. Or, simply allow any pulp to settle to the bottom of the bowl and carefully pour off the juice into another container, leaving the sediment behind.

1. If you are new to canning, or need a refresher, refer to chapter 1 (pages 12–41) for step-by-step guidance and additional information on how to safely can your jelly. Once ready, proceed as follows.
2. Peel the oranges and discard the peels, and then chop the flesh of the oranges.
3. Peel, pit, and dice mangoes (for more information, see "Mango Madness!" on page 63).
4. Combine chopped oranges, diced mangoes, chopped mint and the 1½ cups (355 ml) water in a saucepan. Bring to a boil over high heat, reduce heat, and then simmer, covered, for about 7 to 15 minutes, or until fruit is soft, stirring occasionally. Remove from heat and mash the fruit.
5. Transfer mashed fruit to a damp jelly bag or layered cheesecloth, suspend over a bowl, and allow juice to drip until dripping stops—at least 2 hours. Discard fruit pulp, or save for another use.
6. Prepare your jars, lids, and bands; heat up your canner; and sterilize your jars.
7. Measure 4 cups (946 ml) of fruit juice (if you're short on juice, see "Where's the Juice?" on page 85 for more information) and combine in a saucepan with lime juice and calcium water. Mix well.
8. In a separate bowl, combine sugar and pectin powder. Mix thoroughly and set aside.
9. Bring fruit juice to a full boil over high heat, and then slowly add pectin-sugar mixture, stirring constantly. Continue to stir vigorously for 1 to 2 minutes to dissolve pectin while the jelly comes back up to a boil. Once the jelly returns to a full boil, remove it from the heat.
10. **Can Your Jelly:** Remove jars from canner and ladle hot jelly into hot jars, leaving ¼ inch (6 mm) of headspace. Remove trapped air bubbles, wipe rims with a damp cloth, put on lids and screw bands, and tighten to fingertip tight. Lower filled jars into canner, ensuring jars are not touching each other and are covered with at least 1 to 2 inches (2.5 to 5 cm) of water. Place lid on canner, return to a rolling boil, and process for 10 minutes (adjusting for altitude if necessary). Turn off heat and allow canner to sit untouched for 5 minutes, then remove jars and allow to cool undisturbed for 12 to 24 hours. Confirm that jars have sealed, then store properly.

YIELD: 4 TO 5 HALF-PINT (8-OUNCE, OR 236 ML) JARS

NANA'S FAVORITE DANDELION JELLY

This is a great first-of-the-season jelly to make, as dandelions pop up their bright-yellow heads in the spring, long before anything else is ready (at least in northern climates). My children's grandmother, Nana, is especially fond of this soft-set jelly. Slathered on homemade wheat bread, she and my boys enjoy it on cold winter afternoons. Its delicate flavor and lovely golden color are a welcome reminder of spring days ahead.

4 cups (230 g) loosely packed, very fresh dandelion heads

4¼ cups (1 L) medium-hot water

½ cup (120 ml) lemon juice

4¼ teaspoons (21.3 ml) calcium water*

1 cup (200 g) sugar

4¼ teaspoons (12.8 g) Pomona's pectin powder

For information on how to prepare calcium water, refer to page 22.

PICK WITH CARE

Be sure to use only dandelions that have not been sprayed with pesticides or any other chemicals! This is very important, as you obviously don't want these chemicals in your jelly. Picking dandelions on public property is generally not a good idea, as many towns and cities use pesticides and weed killers in parks and other public areas. Your best bet is to pick dandelions from your own property or a friend's, assuming neither of you uses chemicals on your lawn.

1. If you are new to canning, or need a refresher, refer to chapter 1 (pages 12–41) for step-by-step guidance and additional information on how to safely can your jelly. Once ready, proceed as follows.
2. Prepare your jars, lids, and bands; heat up your canner; and sterilize your jars.
3. Separate the yellow flower petals from their green bases. You can cut off the bases, but pulling the petals out of the green bases works best. Try not to get any green parts in the yellow petals, as the green parts are bitter. Discard the green bases, and reserve the now loose yellow petals.
4. Place loose yellow petals in a heat-tolerant bowl, and pour the 4¼ cups (1 L) of medium-hot water over the flower petals. Cover, and allow petals to steep for 20 to 30 minutes. (Do not over-steep. The longer you steep the petals, the darker the liquid will become, and the darker your jelly will be.)
5. Drain the flowers using a fine mesh strainer or cheesecloth, reserving the infused water and discarding the petals.
6. Measure 4 cups (946 ml) of infused water into a saucepan. (If necessary, add extra water to meet the required measurement.) Add lemon juice and calcium water and mix well.
7. In a separate bowl, combine sugar and pectin powder. Mix thoroughly and set aside.
8. Bring infused water mixture to a full boil over high heat. Slowly add pectin-sugar mixture, stirring constantly. Continue to stir vigorously for 1 to 2 minutes to dissolve pectin while the jelly comes back up to a boil. Once the jelly returns to a full boil, remove it from the heat.
9. **Can Your Jelly:** Remove jars from canner and ladle hot jelly into hot jars, leaving ¼ inch (6 mm) of headspace. Remove trapped air bubbles, wipe rims with a damp cloth, put on lids and screw bands, and tighten to fingertip tight. Lower filled jars into canner, ensuring jars are not touching each other and are covered with at least 1 to 2 inches (2.5 to 5 cm) of water. Place lid on canner, return to a rolling boil, and process for 10 minutes (adjusting for altitude if necessary). Turn off heat and allow canner to sit untouched for 5 minutes, then remove jars and allow to cool undisturbed for 12 to 24 hours. Confirm that jars have sealed, then store properly.

YIELD: 4 TO 5 HALF-PINT (8-OUNCE, OR 236 ML) JARS

APPLE-SAGE JELLY

This jelly is quick and convenient to make at any time of year, as it relies on dried rather than fresh herbs. It has a slightly looser set than some jellies, which makes it an ideal glaze for meats. The assertive flavor of the sage complements roast turkey or pork especially well.

4¼ cups (1 L) unsweetened apple juice

2 tablespoons (4 g) dried sage

¼ cup (60 ml) apple cider vinegar

4 teaspoons (20 ml) calcium water*

¾ cup (150 g) sugar

4 teaspoons (12 g) Pomona's pectin powder

*For information on how to prepare calcium water, refer to page 22.

HALVE IT!

Want to make this recipe for a special dinner but don't have a lot of time? No problem—simply cut the recipe in half! By making just enough to enjoy during a meal or two, you can cut down your prep time significantly as there is no need to use the boiling water bath canner for anything you're planning to eat right away. Simply make the jelly and keep it in the refrigerator until you're ready to use it! For more on refrigerating and freezing jams and jellies, see page 42.

1. If you are new to canning, or need a refresher, refer to chapter 1 (pages 12–41) for step-by-step guidance and additional information on how to safely can your jelly. Once ready, proceed as follows.
2. Prepare your jars, lids, and bands; heat up your canner; and sterilize your jars.
3. Combine apple juice and dried sage in saucepan and bring to a boil. Remove from heat, cover, and allow to steep for 20 minutes.
4. Using a fine mesh strainer or cheesecloth, drain the sage leaves and discard, reserving the infused liquid.
5. Measure out 4 cups (946 ml) of infused liquid (if necessary, add extra unsweetened apple juice to meet the required measurement) and return the measured quantity to the (clean) saucepan. Add vinegar and calcium water and mix well.
6. In a separate bowl, combine sugar and pectin powder. Mix thoroughly and set aside.
7. Bring infused liquid to a full boil over high heat. Slowly add pectin-sugar mixture, stirring constantly. Continue to stir vigorously for 1 to 2 minutes to dissolve pectin while the jelly comes back up to a boil. Once the jelly returns to a full boil, remove it from the heat.
8. **Can Your Jelly:** Remove jars from canner and ladle hot jelly into hot jars, leaving ¼ inch (6 mm) of headspace. Remove trapped air bubbles, wipe rims with a damp cloth, put on lids and screw bands, and tighten to fingertip tight. Lower filled jars into canner, ensuring jars are not touching each other and are covered with at least 1 to 2 inches (2.5 to 5 cm) of water. Place lid on canner, return to a rolling boil, and process for 10 minutes (adjusting for altitude if necessary). Turn off heat and allow canner to sit untouched for 5 minutes, then remove jars and allow to cool undisturbed for 12 to 24 hours. Confirm that jars have sealed, then store properly.

YIELD: 4 TO 5 HALF-PINT (8-OUNCE, OR 236 ML) JARS

PEACH-CHAMPAGNE JELLY

Infused with the heady essence of ripe peaches and laced with champagne, this delicate, golden jelly makes a lovely gift. Served alongside scones or atop light and airy meringues, it's a sophisticated addition to a special brunch—though it likely won't last long!

3 pounds (1.4 kg) ripe peaches*

1 cup (235 ml) water

1 cup (235 ml) champagne

¼ cup (60 ml) lemon juice

4 teaspoons (20 ml) calcium water**

1 cup (200 g) sugar

4 teaspoons (12 g) Pomona's pectin powder

*Not sure how much fruit to purchase? See "Measuring Up!" on page 26.

**For information on how to prepare calcium water, refer to page 22.

PIT AND PEEL ... OR NOT?

Because jelly making requires only the juice of the fruit, peeling, pitting, coring, and de-stemming are not essential. Skipping this step is certainly quicker, so the choice is yours. I prefer to remove pits, peels, cores, and stems, however, as it allows me to use the fruit pulp afterward for something else.

1. If you are new to canning, or need a refresher, refer to chapter 1 (pages 12–41) for step-by-step guidance and additional information on how to safely can your jelly. Once ready, proceed as follows.
2. Peel and remove pits from peaches (if desired; for more information, see "Pit and Peel … Or Not?" below), and then chop. Combine chopped peaches in a saucepan with the 1 cup (235 ml) of water. Bring to a boil over high heat, reduce heat, and simmer, covered, for 7 to 15 minutes, or until peaches are soft, stirring occasionally. Remove from heat and mash peaches.
3. Transfer mashed fruit to a damp jelly bag or layered cheesecloth, suspend over a bowl, and allow juice to drip until dripping stops—at least 2 hours. Discard fruit pulp or save for another use.
4. Prepare your jars, lids, and bands; heat up your canner; and sterilize your jars.
5. Measure out 3 cups (710 ml) of the fruit juice (if you're short on juice, see "Where's the Juice?" on page 85 for more information) and combine in a saucepan with champagne, lemon juice, and calcium water.
6. In a separate bowl, combine sugar and pectin powder. Mix thoroughly and set aside.
7. Bring juice mixture to a full boil over high heat, and then slowly add pectin-sugar mixture, stirring constantly. Continue to stir vigorously for 1 to 2 minutes to dissolve pectin while the jelly comes back up to a boil. Once the jelly returns to a full boil, remove it from the heat.
8. **Can Your Jelly:** Remove jars from canner and ladle hot jelly into hot jars, leaving ¼ inch (6 mm) of headspace. Remove trapped air bubbles, wipe rims with a damp cloth, put on lids and screw bands, and tighten to fingertip tight. Lower filled jars into canner, ensuring jars are not touching each other and are covered with at least 1 to 2 inches (2.5 to 5 cm) of water. Place lid on canner, return to a rolling boil, and process for 10 minutes (adjusting for altitude if necessary). Turn off heat and allow canner to sit untouched for 5 minutes, then remove jars and allow to cool undisturbed for 12 to 24 hours. Confirm that jars have sealed, then store properly.

YIELD: 4 HALF-PINT (8-OUNCE, OR 236 ML) JARS

ROSEMARY-WINE JELLY

This jelly calls for fresh herbs, and if you're fortunate enough to have a potted rosemary plant that you can bring indoors in the winter (as many herb-lovers do), you can make this jelly year-round. It makes a delicious glaze for roasted meats, and it is a perfect accompaniment to winter holiday meals and on other special occasions.

1 cup (60 g) coarsely chopped, firmly packed fresh rosemary leaves and stems

4¼ cups (1.1 L) dry white wine

½ cup (120 ml) white wine vinegar

4 teaspoons (20 ml) calcium water*

1 cup (200 g) sugar

4 teaspoons (12 g) Pomona's pectin powder

*For information on how to prepare calcium water, refer to page 22.

1. If you are new to canning, or need a refresher, refer to chapter 1 (pages 12–41) for step-by-step guidance and additional information on how to safely can your jelly. Once ready, proceed as follows.
2. Prepare your jars, lids, and bands; heat up your canner; and sterilize your jars.
3. Combine chopped fresh rosemary and the dry white wine in a saucepan and bring to a boil. Remove from heat, cover, and allow to steep for 20 minutes.
4. Using a fine mesh strainer or cheesecloth, drain the rosemary and discard, reserving the infused liquid.
5. Measure 4 cups (946 ml) of infused liquid (if necessary, add extra dry white wine to meet the required measurement) and return the measured quantity to the (clean) saucepan. Add vinegar and calcium water and mix well.
6. In a separate bowl, combine sugar and pectin powder. Mix thoroughly and set aside.
7. Bring infused liquid to a full boil over high heat. Slowly add pectin-sugar mixture, stirring constantly. Continue to stir vigorously for 1 to 2 minutes to dissolve pectin while the jelly comes back up to a boil. Once the jelly returns to a full boil, remove it from the heat.
8. **Can Your Jelly:** Remove jars from canner and ladle hot jelly into hot jars, leaving ¼ inch (6 mm) of headspace. Remove trapped air bubbles, wipe rims with a damp cloth, put on lids and screw bands, and tighten to fingertip tight. Lower filled jars into canner, ensuring jars are not touching each other and are covered with at least 1 to 2 inches (2.5 to 5 cm) of water. Place lid on canner, return to a rolling boil, and process for 10 minutes (adjusting for altitude if necessary). Turn off heat and allow canner to sit untouched for 5 minutes, then remove jars and allow to cool undisturbed for 12 to 24 hours. Confirm that jars have sealed, then store properly.

YIELD: 4 TO 5 HALF-PINT (8-OUNCE, OR 236 ML) JARS

TOUGH STUFF!

Mature rosemary plants often have tough stems that can be difficult to cut. Trying to chop these stems with a knife as you would other herbs can be an exercise in frustration. Instead, use scissors—they work beautifully!

STRAWBERRY-BALSAMIC JELLY

I adore the flavor combination of strawberry and balsamic, and this beautiful, dark-red jelly is particularly intriguing because, with just a small amount of balsamic vinegar, it straddles the line between a straight-ahead sweet jelly and a savory, more complex jelly. It's delicious atop scones at brunch, and it is equally good served with your favorite cheese in the evening as an appetizer.

4 pounds (1.8 kg) strawberries*

½ cup (120 ml) water

¼ cup (60 ml) balsamic vinegar

4 teaspoons (20 ml) calcium water**

1 cup (200 g) sugar

4 teaspoons (12 g) Pomona's pectin powder

*Not sure how much fruit to purchase? See "Measuring Up!" on page 26.

**For information on how to prepare your calcium water, refer to page 24.

COOK OR JUST CRUSH?

When you're dealing with juicy fruit such as strawberries, raspberries, or blackberries, it's not essential to cook your fruit with water before juicing them. You can simply mash fresh berries and then hang them in your jelly bag or cheesecloth to drip. It's your choice. I prefer to cook berries first —with a tiny bit of water for just a couple of minutes—as I find it gets the juices flowing more easily.

1. If you are new to canning, or need a refresher, refer to chapter 1 (pages 12–41) for step-by-step guidance and additional information on how to safely can your jelly. Once ready, proceed as follows.
2. Rinse strawberries and remove stems. Combine strawberries in a saucepan with the ½ cup (120 ml) water, and bring to a boil over high heat. Reduce heat, and simmer, covered, for 2 to 4 minutes, stirring frequently. Remove from heat and mash strawberries. (Or, for an alternative method, see tip below.)
3. Transfer mashed strawberries to a damp jelly bag or layered cheesecloth, suspend over a bowl, and allow juice to drip until it stops—at least 2 hours. Discard fruit pulp, or save for another use.
4. Prepare your jars, lids, and bands; heat up your canner; and sterilize your jars.
5. Measure 4 cups (946 ml) of the strawberry juice, and pour into a saucepan. Add balsamic vinegar and calcium water and mix well.
6. In a separate bowl, combine the sugar and the pectin powder. Mix thoroughly and set aside.
7. Bring the juice mixture to a full boil over high heat, and then slowly add the pectin-sugar mixture, stirring constantly. Continue to stir vigorously for 1 to 2 minutes to thoroughly dissolve pectin as the jelly comes back up to a boil. Once the jelly returns to a full boil, remove it from the heat.
8. **Can Your Jelly:** Remove jars from canner and ladle hot jelly into hot jars, leaving ¼ inch (6 mm) of headspace. Remove trapped air bubbles, wipe rims with a damp cloth, put on lids and screw bands, and tighten to fingertip tight. Lower filled jars into canner, ensuring jars are not touching each other and are covered with at least 1 to 2 inches (2.5 to 5 cm) of water. Place lid on canner, return to a rolling boil, and process for 10 minutes (adjusting for altitude if necessary). Turn off heat and allow canner to sit untouched for 5 minutes, then remove jars and allow to cool undisturbed for 12 to 24 hours. Confirm that jars have sealed, then store properly.

YIELD: 4 TO 5 HALF-PINT (8-OUNCE, OR 236 ML) JARS

WHERE'S THE JUICE?

What do you do if your jelly bag is done dripping, but you don't have enough juice? Slowly pour extra hot water—a very small amount at a time—onto the fruit pulp in the jelly bag, making sure it mixes with the fruit and drips out slowly, until you have the quantity of juice needed. Alternatively, you can dump the fruit pulp back in the pot with some extra water, cook for a few minutes, and then return the fruit to the jelly bag or cheesecloth to continue dripping until you have enough juice.

BLACKBERRY-WINE JELLY

I love to pick blackberries in the woods in the late summer, and this jelly is a wonderful way to enjoy them. The wine adds a light, refreshing touch to this jelly. If, by chance, you ate too many berries while picking (as I usually do) and don't have quite enough berries for this recipe, you can decrease the amount of juice just a bit and increase the wine—just remember that the total quantity of the juice–wine mixture should be 4 cups (946 ml).

3 pounds (1.4 kg) blackberries*

¾ cup (175 ml) water

1 cup (235 ml) dry white wine

¼ cup (60 ml) lemon juice

4 teaspoons (20 ml) calcium water**

1½ cups (300 g) sugar

4 teaspoons (12 g) Pomona's pectin powder

Not sure how much fruit to purchase? See "Measuring Up!" on page 26.

**For information on how to prepare calcium water, refer to page 22.*

1. If you are new to canning, or need a refresher, refer to chapter 1 (pages 12–41) for step-by-step guidance and additional information on how to safely can your jelly. Once ready, proceed as follows.
2. Rinse blackberries, remove stems, and combine in a saucepan with the ¾ cup (175 ml) of water. Bring to a boil over high heat, reduce heat, and simmer, covered, for 2 to 4 minutes, stirring occasionally. Remove from heat and mash blackberries. (Or, for an alternative method, see tip below.)
3. Transfer mashed berries to a damp jelly bag or layered cheesecloth, suspend over a bowl, and allow juice to drip until dripping stops—at least 2 hours. Discard fruit pulp or save for another use.
4. Prepare your jars, lids, and bands; heat up your canner; and sterilize your jars.
5. Measure out 3 cups (710 ml) of the fruit juice (if you're short on juice, see "Where's the Juice?" on page 85 for more information) and combine in a saucepan with dry white wine, lemon juice, and calcium water.
6. In a separate bowl, combine sugar and pectin powder. Mix thoroughly and set aside.
7. Bring juice mixture to a full boil over high heat, and then slowly add pectin-sugar mixture, stirring constantly. Continue to stir vigorously for 1 to 2 minutes to dissolve pectin while the jelly comes back up to a boil. Once the jelly returns to a full boil, remove it from the heat.
8. **Can Your Jelly:** Remove jars from canner and ladle hot jelly into hot jars, leaving ¼ inch (6 mm) of headspace. Remove trapped air bubbles, wipe rims with a damp cloth, put on lids and screw bands, and tighten to fingertip tight. Lower filled jars into canner, ensuring jars are not touching each other and are covered with at least 1 to 2 inches (2.5 to 5 cm) of water. Place lid on canner, return to a rolling boil, and process for 10 minutes (adjusting for altitude if necessary). Turn off heat and allow canner to sit untouched for 5 minutes, then remove jars and allow to cool undisturbed for 12 to 24 hours. Confirm that jars have sealed, then store properly.

YIELD: 4 TO 5 HALF-PINT (8-OUNCE, OR 236 ML) JARS

LAVENDER JELLY

Adapted from a recipe by jelly-maker Kelli Menzen of Crossroads Bakeshop in Doylestown, Pennsylvania, this delicious, complex jelly is a refreshing change of pace from other jellies in that it's made from infused lavender water, rather than fruit juice. It's not purple; rather, it's a lovely golden brown. It is delightful on scones for afternoon tea. Lavender buds are available in the herb section of many natural food stores.

4¼ cups (1 L) hot (not boiling) water

½ cup (19 g) dried lavender buds

½ cup (120 ml) lemon juice

4¼ teaspoons (21 ml) calcium water*

1¾ cups (350 g) sugar

4¼ teaspoons (12.8 g) Pomona's pectin powder

For information on how to prepare calcium water, refer to page 22.

1. If you are new to canning, or need a refresher, refer to chapter 1 (pages 12–41) for step-by-step guidance and additional information on how to safely can your jelly. Once ready, proceed as follows.
2. Prepare your jars, lids, and bands; heat up your canner; and sterilize your jars.
3. Place lavender buds in a heat-proof bowl and pour the 4¼ cups (1 L) hot (not boiling) water over them. Cover and allow to steep for 15 to 20 minutes.
4. Using a fine mesh strainer, drain and discard the lavender buds, reserving the infused liquid.
5. Measure 4 cups (946 ml) of the infused liquid (if necessary, add extra water to meet the required measurement) and combine in a saucepan with lemon juice and calcium water.
6. In a separate bowl, combine sugar and pectin powder. Mix thoroughly and set aside.
7. Bring infused lavender mixture to a full boil over high heat, and then slowly add pectin-sugar mixture, stirring constantly. Continue to stir vigorously for 1 to 2 minutes to dissolve pectin while the jelly comes back up to a boil. Once the jelly returns to a full boil, remove it from the heat.
8. **Can Your Jelly:** Remove jars from canner and ladle hot jelly into hot jars, leaving ¼ inch (6 mm) of headspace. Remove trapped air bubbles, wipe rims with a damp cloth, put on lids and screw bands, and tighten to fingertip tight. Lower filled jars into canner, ensuring jars are not touching each other and are covered with at least 1 to 2 inches (2.5 to 5 cm) of water. Place lid on canner, return to a rolling boil, and process for 10 minutes (adjusting for altitude if necessary). Turn off heat and allow canner to sit untouched for 5 minutes, then remove jars and allow to cool undisturbed for 12 to 24 hours. Confirm that jars have sealed, then store properly.

YIELD: 4 TO 5 HALF-PINT (8-OUNCE, OR 236 ML) JARS

KEEP IT SHORT AND SWEET!

Be careful that you don't oversteep the lavender or your jelly may be bitter. You'll have plenty of lovely lavender flavor with 15 to 20 minutes of steeping.

CRANBERRY-HABANERO JELLY

Hot pepper aficionados will appreciate the distinctive kick of this habanero pepper jelly, yet it's mild enough that it can be enjoyed by those who like only very small amounts of heat. The cranberries add a brilliant red hue to this translucent, yellow-flecked jelly. Served with cream cheese and crackers, it makes a gorgeous and spicy addition to any appetizer table. Remember, for canning safety, do not increase the quantity of any peppers in this recipe.

¼ cup (38 g) finely chopped cranberries

1¼ cups (150 g) seeded, finely diced yellow bell pepper

2 teaspoons (6 g) seeded, minced habanero pepper

1½ cups (355 ml) white vinegar

2½ cups (500 g) sugar, divided

2 teaspoons (6 g) Pomona's pectin powder

2 teaspoons (10 ml) calcium water*

For information on how to prepare calcium water, refer to page 22.

1. If you are new to canning, or need a refresher, refer to chapter 1 (pages 12–41) for step-by-step guidance and additional information on how to safely can your jelly. Once ready, proceed as follows.
2. Prepare your jars, lids, and bands; heat up your canner; and sterilize your jars.
3. Combine chopped cranberries, diced yellow pepper, minced habanero pepper, and vinegar in a saucepan. Cover, bring to a boil, and then reduce heat and simmer, still covered, for 5 minutes. Remove from heat.
4. In a separate bowl, combine pectin powder with ½ cup (100 g) of the sugar. Mix thoroughly and set aside.
5. Add calcium water to the pepper mixture, mix well, and return the mixture to a full boil over high heat. Slowly add pectin-sugar mixture, stirring constantly. Continue to stir vigorously for 1 to 2 minutes to dissolve pectin while the jelly returns to a boil. After the pectin is *fully* dissolved, add the remaining quantity of sugar and stir to dissolve it. Once sugar is dissolved, and the jelly returns to a full boil, remove it from the heat.
6. **Can Your Jelly:** Remove jars from canner and ladle hot jelly into hot jars, leaving ¼ inch (6 mm) of headspace. Remove trapped air bubbles, wipe rims with a damp cloth, put on lids and screw bands, and tighten to fingertip tight. Lower filled jars into canner, ensuring jars are not touching each other and are covered with at least 1 to 2 inches (2.5 to 5 cm) of water. Place lid on canner, return to a rolling boil, and process for 10 minutes (adjusting for altitude if necessary). Turn off heat and allow canner to sit untouched for 5 minutes, then remove jars and allow to cool undisturbed for 12 to 24 hours. Confirm that jars have sealed, then store properly.

YIELD: 3 TO 4 HALF-PINT (8-OUNCE, OR 236 ML) JARS

HOLY HOTNESS!

Habanero peppers are about as hot as they come, and getting even a little on your skin can be quite painful. Always wear gloves when working with them, do not let them come in contact with any part of your body (especially your eyes). Use common sense to keep safe and pain free!

JALAPEÑO-CONFETTI JELLY

The colorful bell peppers and the tequila add a festive flair to this lovely pepper jelly, adapted from a recipe by jelly-maker Denise Satterfield. This jelly has a little bit of a bite, and a slightly softer set than some jellies, and makes an excellent glaze for grilled meats and vegetables. Or, try a dollop of it on a hunk of warm cornbread—delicious! For canning safety, remember not to increase the quantity of any peppers in this recipe, and be sure to use bottled lime juice.

1 cup (120 g) seeded, finely diced yellow, red, or orange bell peppers (or a combination of the three)

½ cup (72 g) seeded, finely chopped jalapeño peppers

1 cup (235 ml) red wine vinegar

½ cup (120 ml) lime juice

2½ cups (500 g) sugar, divided

2 teaspoons (6 g) Pomona's pectin powder

1 tablespoon (15 ml) tequila (optional)

2 teaspoons (10 ml) calcium water*

*For information on how to prepare calcium water, refer to page 22.

1. If you are new to canning, or need a refresher, refer to chapter 1 (pages 12–41) for step-by-step guidance and additional information on how to safely can your jelly. Once ready, proceed as follows.
2. Prepare your jars, lids, and bands; heat up your canner; and sterilize your jars.
3. In a large saucepan, combine bell pepper, jalapeño pepper, vinegar, and lime juice. Cover, bring the mixture to a boil, reduce heat, and simmer, still covered, for 5 minutes. Remove from heat.
4. In a separate bowl, combine pectin powder with ½ cup (100 g) of the sugar. Mix thoroughly and set aside.
5. Add tequila and calcium water to the pepper mixture, mix well, and return the mixture to a full boil over high heat. Slowly add pectin-sugar mixture, stirring constantly. Continue to stir vigorously for 1 to 2 minutes to dissolve pectin while the jelly comes back up to a boil. After the pectin is *fully* dissolved, add the remaining quantity of sugar and stir to dissolve it. Once sugar is dissolved, and the jelly returns to a full boil, remove it from the heat.
6. **Can Your Jelly:** Remove jars from canner and ladle hot jelly into hot jars, leaving ¼ inch (6 mm) of headspace. Remove trapped air bubbles, wipe rims with a damp cloth, put on lids and screw bands, and tighten to fingertip tight. Lower filled jars into canner, ensuring jars are not touching each other and are covered with at least 1 to 2 inches (2.5 to 5 cm) of water. Place lid on canner, return to a rolling boil, and process for 10 minutes (adjusting for altitude if necessary). Turn off heat and allow canner to sit untouched for 5 minutes, then remove jars and allow to cool undisturbed for 12 to 24 hours. Confirm that jars have sealed, then store properly.

YIELD: 3 TO 4 HALF-PINT (8-OUNCE, OR 236 ML) JARS

PULSE IT!

If you're in a hurry, you can chop your peppers in a food processor. Remove seeds and cut peppers into roughly 1-inch (2.5 cm) long pieces by hand first, and then use your food processor to chop them down to roughly ⅛ inch (3 mm). And remember, jalapeños are hot, so be sure to wear gloves to protect your hands while handling them!

MAPLE-PEAR JELLY

Pears never overstate themselves, and in my mind, their beauty lies in the subtle nature and quiet complexity of their flavors. Combined with a touch of the deep, earthy intensity of real maple syrup, this jelly captures the essence of both pear and maple at their best.

4 pounds (1.8 kg) ripe pears*

1¾ cups (414 ml) water

¼ cup (60 ml) lemon juice

4 teaspoons (20 ml) calcium water**

½ cup (120 ml) maple syrup (for more information, see "Go for the Real Thing!" on page 182)

5 teaspoons (15 g) Pomona's pectin powder

*Not sure how much fruit to purchase? See "Measuring Up!" on page 26.

**For information on how to prepare calcium water, refer to page 22.

WHERE'S THE JUICE?

What do you do if your jelly bag is done dripping, but you don't have enough juice? Slowly pour extra hot water—a very small amount at a time—onto the fruit pulp in the jelly bag, making sure it mixes with the fruit and drips out slowly, until you have the quantity of juice needed. Alternatively, you can dump the fruit pulp back in the pot with some extra water, cook for a few minutes, and then return the fruit to the jelly bag or cheesecloth to continue dripping until you have enough juice.

1. If you are new to canning, or need a refresher, refer to chapter 1 (pages 12–41) for step-by-step guidance and additional information on how to safely can your jelly. Once ready, proceed as follows.
2. Peel and core pears (if desired; for more information, see "Pit and Peel … Or Not?" on page 94), and then chop. Combine chopped pears in a saucepan with the 1¾ cups (414 ml) of water. Bring to a boil over high heat, reduce heat, and simmer, covered, for 7 to 15 minutes, or until pears are soft, stirring occasionally. Remove from heat and mash pears.
3. Transfer mashed fruit to a damp jelly bag or layered cheesecloth, suspend over a bowl, and allow juice to drip until dripping stops—at least 2 hours. Discard fruit pulp or save for another use.
4. Prepare your jars, lids, and bands; heat up your canner; and sterilize your jars.
5. Measure 4 cups (946 ml) of the fruit juice, and combine in a saucepan with lemon juice and calcium water.
6. In a separate bowl, combine maple syrup and pectin powder. Mix thoroughly and set aside.
7. Bring fruit juice mixture to a full boil over high heat, and then slowly add pectin–maple syrup mixture, stirring constantly. Continue to stir vigorously for 1 to 2 minutes to dissolve pectin while the jelly comes back up to a boil. Once the jelly returns to a full boil, remove it from the heat.
8. **Can Your Jelly:** Remove jars from canner and ladle hot jelly into hot jars, leaving ¼ inch (6 mm) of headspace. Remove trapped air bubbles, wipe rims with a damp cloth, put on lids and screw bands, and tighten to fingertip tight. Lower filled jars into canner, ensuring jars are not touching each other and are covered with at least 1 to 2 inches (2.5 to 5 cm) of water. Place lid on canner, return to a rolling boil, and process for 10 minutes (adjusting for altitude if necessary). Turn off heat and allow canner to sit untouched for 5 minutes, then remove jars and allow to cool undisturbed for 12 to 24 hours. Confirm that jars have sealed, then store properly.

YIELD: 4 TO 5 HALF-PINT (8-OUNCE, OR 236 ML) JARS

Chapter 4

PRESERVES

||||||||||||||||||||||||||||||||||||||||||||||||||||||||||||||||||||||||||||||||||||||||||||||||||||||||||

In my mind, preserves are the most luxurious—perhaps even most deca-dent—of all the jelled goods. With whole, small fruits or uniform chunks of fruits, suspended in a jelled syrup, they straddle the line between a delicious but eminently functional jam and an elegant specialty dessert item. Preserves tend to have a slightly looser set than jams, and because of the relative translucence of the jelled syrup, incorporating additional colorful ingredients—thinly sliced lemon peel, for example—can add tremendously to the visual appeal of the preserve. Other specialty items, such as liqueurs, are excellent in preserves as well. Whether you prefer simple preserves, or preserves in a more glamorous form, there are many options to choose from in this chapter. And, either way, they're delicious.

SIMPLE CLASSIC: PEACH PRESERVES

Ripe, in-season, just-picked peaches say summer to me more than just about any fruit, and they're so naturally sweet and juicy that they need little else to really sing. This easy, classic preserve allows the luscious flavor of peaches to really shine through, showing them off at their simplest and most glorious. Try this preserve as a filling for *crostata* (an Italian baked tart) for a delightful treat!

IIIIIIIIIIIIIIIIIIIIIIIIIIIIIIIIIIIIIIIIIIIIIIIIIIIIIIIIIIIIIIIIIIIIIIIIIIIIIIIIIIIIIIIIIIIIIIIIIIIIIIIIIIIIIIIIIIIIIIIIIIIIIIIII

2¾ pounds (1.2 kg) ripe peaches*

¼ cup (60 ml) water

¼ cup (60 ml) lemon juice

3½ teaspoons (17.5 ml) calcium water**

1 cup (200 g) sugar

2½ teaspoons (7.5 g) Pomona's pectin powder

Not sure how much fruit to purchase? See "Measuring Up!" on page 26.

**For information on how to prepare calcium water, refer to page 22.*

1. If you are new to canning, or need a refresher, refer to chapter 1 (pages 12–41) for step-by-step guidance and additional information on how to safely can your preserves. Once ready, proceed as follows.
2. Prepare your jars, lids, and bands; heat up your canner; and sterilize your jars.
3. Peel and remove pits from peaches, and then cut peaches into uniform-size pieces. (For more information, see "How to Skin a Peach" on page 58.)
4. Combine peaches and the ¼ cup (60 ml) of water in a saucepan. Bring to a boil over high heat, reduce heat, and simmer, covered, for 3 to 5 minutes, or until fruit is soft (but still retains its shape), stirring occasionally. Remove from heat.
5. Measure 4 cups (946 ml) of the cooked mixture (saving any extra for another use), and return the measured quantity to the saucepan. Add lemon juice and calcium water and mix well.
6. In a separate bowl, combine sugar and pectin powder. Mix thoroughly and set aside.
7. Bring peach mixture to a full boil over high heat. Slowly add pectin-sugar mixture, stirring constantly. Continue to stir vigorously for 1 to 2 minutes to dissolve pectin while the preserves come back up to a boil. Once the preserves return to a full boil, remove the pan from the heat.
8. **Can Your Preserves:** Remove jars from canner and ladle hot preserves into hot jars, leaving ¼ inch (6 mm) of headspace. Remove trapped air bubbles, wipe rims with a damp cloth, put on lids and screw bands, and tighten to fingertip tight. Lower filled jars into canner, ensuring jars are not touching each other and are covered with at least 1 to 2 inches (2.5 to 5 cm) of water. Place lid on canner, return to a rolling boil, and process for 10 minutes (adjusting for altitude if necessary). Turn off heat and allow canner to sit untouched for 5 minutes, then remove jars and allow to cool undisturbed for 12 to 24 hours. Confirm that jars have sealed, then store properly.

YIELD: 4 TO 5 HALF-PINT (8-OUNCE, OR 236 ML) JARS

IIIIIIIIIIIIIIIIIIIIIIIIIIIIIIIIIIIIIIIIIIIIIIIIIIIIIIIIIIIIIIIIIIIIII

CUSTOMIZE IT!

If you're looking for something new, try spicing it up! At the same time that you add the calcium water, add up to 1 teaspoon (2.5 g) of ground ginger, cardamom, cloves, cinnamon, nutmeg, or allspice. Or, you can mix and match these spices—just be sure that the total spice quantity does not exceed 1 teaspoon (2.5 g).

IIIIIIIIIIIIIIIIIIIIIIIIIIIIIIIIIIIIIIIIIIIIIIIIIIIIIIIIIIIIIIII

SIMPLE CLASSIC: RASPBERRY PRESERVES

This simple, classic preserve highlights raspberries at their absolute best. Raspberries are so delicate that they tend to break apart when cooked, so this preserve is similar to jam in texture. Spread this delectable preserve on warm muffins with a bit of butter, or enjoy it as a filling for thumbprints (pictured on page 74), turnovers, or other pastries!

|||||||||||||||||||||||||||||||||||||||||||||||||||||||||||||||||||||||||||||||||||||||||||||||||||||||||||||||||||||||||||

2¼ pounds (1 kg) raspberries*

¼ cup (60 ml) water

2 teaspoons (10 ml) calcium water**

1½ cups (300 g) sugar

2 teaspoons (6 g) Pomona's pectin powder

*Not sure how much fruit to purchase? See "Measuring Up!" on page 26.

**For information on how to prepare calcium water, refer to page 22.

1. If you are new to canning, or need a refresher, refer to chapter 1 (pages 12–41) for step-by-step guidance and additional information on how to safely can your preserves. Once ready, proceed as follows.
2. Prepare your jars, lids, and bands; heat up your canner; and sterilize your jars.
3. Carefully pick through raspberries, removing stems and any damaged parts. Rinse raspberries only if necessary. Combine in a large saucepan with the ¼ cup (60 ml) water. Bring to a boil over high heat, reduce heat, and simmer, covered, for 2 minutes or until raspberries release their juices, stirring occasionally and gently (don't worry if the berries break apart). Remove from heat.
4. Measure 4 cups (946 ml) of the cooked raspberries (saving any extra for another use) and return the measured quantity to the saucepan. Add calcium water and mix well.
5. In a separate bowl, combine sugar and pectin powder. Mix thoroughly and set aside.
6. Bring raspberry mixture back to a full boil over high heat. Slowly add the pectin-sugar mixture, stirring constantly. Continue to stir vigorously for 1 to 2 minutes to dissolve pectin while the preserves come back up to a boil. Once the preserves return to a full boil, remove the pan from the heat.
7. **Can Your Preserves:** Remove jars from canner and ladle hot preserves into hot jars, leaving ¼ inch (6 mm) of headspace. Remove trapped air bubbles, wipe rims with a damp cloth, put on lids and screw bands, and tighten to fingertip tight. Lower filled jars into canner, ensuring jars are not touching each other and are covered with at least 1 to 2 inches (2.5 to 5 cm) of water. Place lid on canner, return to a rolling boil, and process for 10 minutes (adjusting for altitude if necessary). Turn off heat and allow canner to sit untouched for 5 minutes, then remove jars and allow to cool undisturbed for 12 to 24 hours. Confirm that jars have sealed, then store properly.

YIELD: 4 TO 5 HALF-PINT (8-OUNCE, OR 236 ML) JARS

||||||||||||||||||||||||||||||||||||||||||||||||||||||||||

CUSTOMIZE IT!

If you're looking for something new, try spicing it up! At the same time that you add the calcium water, add up to 1 teaspoon (2.5 g) of ground ginger, cardamom, cloves, cinnamon, nutmeg, or allspice. Or you can mix and match these spices—just be sure that the total spice quantity does not exceed 1 teaspoon (2.5 g).

|||||||||||||||||||||||||||||||||||||||||||||||||||||||||||||

VANILLA-PLUM PRESERVES

Fresh, sweet, in-season plums have a wonderful depth and complexity, and the smooth richness of vanilla in this preserve really highlights this. For a luscious, visually stunning dessert, use these preserves layered with mascarpone cheese in a parfait!

||||||||||||||||||||||||||||||||||||||||||||||||||||||||||||||||||||||||||||||||||||||||||||||||||||||||||||||||||||||||||||||||||||||

2½ pounds (1.1 kg) ripe, sweet plums*

¼ cup (60 ml) water

1 vanilla bean

¼ cup (60 ml) lemon juice

3½ teaspoons (17.5 ml) calcium water**

1½ cups (300 g) sugar

2½ teaspoons (7.5 g) Pomona's pectin powder

Not sure how much fruit to purchase? See "Measuring Up!" on page 26.

**For information on how to prepare calcium water, refer to page 22.*

||||||||||||||||||||||||||||||||||||||||||||||||||||||||||||||||||||||||||||||||

CUSTOMIZE IT!

If you prefer a less-processed sugar, such as turbinado (raw sugar), you can use that instead of regular white sugar. Just be sure to pulse it in a food processor a few times to make the granules fine enough that you'll be able to mix the pectin into the sugar effectively.

1. If you are new to canning, or need a refresher, refer to chapter 1 (pages 12–41) for step-by-step guidance and additional information on how to safely can your preserves. Once ready, proceed as follows.
2. Prepare your jars, lids, and bands; heat up your canner; and sterilize your jars.
3. Rinse plums, remove stems, and slice in half. Remove pits, and cut into uniform pieces. (For more information, see "To Peel or Not to Peel?" on page 76.)
4. Combine plums and the ¼ cup (60 ml) of water in a saucepan. Bring to a boil over high heat, reduce heat, and simmer, covered, for 4 to 6 minutes or until fruit is soft, stirring occasionally. Remove from heat.
5. Measure 4 cups (946 ml) of the cooked plums (saving any extra for another use), and return the measured quantity to the saucepan. Using a paring knife, slice the vanilla bean in half lengthwise and scrape out the seeds. Add the vanilla seeds and the bean pod itself to the plum mixture. Add lemon juice and calcium water and mix well.
6. In a separate bowl, combine sugar and pectin powder. Mix thoroughly and set aside.
7. Bring plum mixture back to a full boil over high heat. Slowly add pectin-sugar mixture, stirring constantly. Continue to stir vigorously for 1 to 2 minutes to dissolve pectin while the preserves come back up to a boil. Once the preserves return to a full boil, remove the pan from the heat. Using tongs, carefully remove the vanilla bean pod and discard.
8. **Can Your Preserves:** Remove jars from canner and ladle hot preserves into hot jars, leaving ¼ inch (6 mm) of headspace. Remove trapped air bubbles, wipe rims with a damp cloth, put on lids and screw bands, and tighten to fingertip tight. Lower filled jars into canner, ensuring jars are not touching each other and are covered with at least 1 to 2 inches (2.5 to 5 cm) of water. Place lid on canner, return to a rolling boil, and process for 10 minutes (adjusting for altitude if necessary). Turn off heat and allow canner to sit untouched for 5 minutes, then remove jars and allow to cool undisturbed for 12 to 24 hours. Confirm that jars have sealed, then store properly.

YIELD: 4 TO 5 HALF-PINT (8-OUNCE, OR 236 ML) JARS

||||||||||||||||||||||||||||||||||||||||||||||||||||||||||||||||||

CHERRY-PORT PRESERVES

Combining luscious, sweet cherry flavor with the depth and complexity of port wine, this gorgeous, deep-red preserve is just heavenly. It's a perfect addition to a special-occasion brunch and makes a wonderful gift. Or, spoon it on a slice of lemon pound cake and top with fresh whipped cream for a simple and elegant dessert.

1¾ pounds (794 g) sweet cherries*

½ cup (120 ml) water

¾ cup (175 ml) port wine

¼ cup (60 ml) lemon juice

2 teaspoons (10 ml) calcium water**

1 cup (200 g) sugar

1½ teaspoons (4.5 g) Pomona's pectin powder

*Not sure how much fruit to purchase? See "Measuring Up!" on page 26.

**For information on how to prepare calcium water, refer to page 22.

1. If you are new to canning, or need a refresher, refer to chapter 1 (pages 12–41) for step-by-step guidance and additional information on how to safely can your preserves. Once ready, proceed as follows.
2. Prepare your jars, lids, and bands; heat up your canner; and sterilize your jars.
3. Rinse cherries, remove stems, and then slice in half and remove pits. (For more information, see "Painless Pitting" on page 70.)
4. Combine cherry halves with the ½ cup (120 ml) of water in a saucepan. Bring to a boil over high heat, reduce heat, and simmer, covered, for 5 minutes, stirring occasionally. Remove from heat, add port, and mix well.
5. Measure 4 cups (946 ml) of the cherry mixture (saving any extra for another use), and return the measured quantity to the saucepan. Add lemon juice and calcium water, and mix well.
6. In a separate bowl, combine sugar and pectin powder. Mix thoroughly and set aside.
7. Bring fruit mixture back to a full boil over high heat. Slowly add pectin-sugar mixture, stirring constantly. Continue to stir vigorously for 1 to 2 minutes to dissolve pectin while the preserves come back up to a boil. Once the mixture returns to a full boil, remove it from the heat.
8. **Can Your Preserves:** Remove jars from canner and ladle hot preserves into hot jars, leaving ¼ inch (6 mm) of headspace. Remove trapped air bubbles, wipe rims with a damp cloth, put on lids and screw bands, and tighten to fingertip tight. Lower filled jars into canner, ensuring jars are not touching each other and are covered with at least 1 to 2 inches (2.5 to 5 cm) of water. Place lid on canner, return to a rolling boil, and process for 10 minutes (adjusting for altitude if necessary). Turn off heat and allow canner to sit untouched for 5 minutes, then remove jars and allow to cool undisturbed for 12 to 24 hours. Confirm that jars have sealed, then store properly.

YIELD: 4 TO 5 HALF-PINT (8-OUNCE, OR 236 ML) JARS

CUSTOMIZE IT!

Looking for something new? Try using lime juice in place of the lemon juice in this recipe.

LEMON-PEAR PRESERVES with CARDAMOM

In this delightful autumn preserve, sweet slices of pear are suspended in a subtly spiced, lemony jelled syrup. Its delightful fragrance is due in part to the lemon zest—the finely grated exterior part of the lemon. Zesting is easy to do: Leaving the fruit whole, and using a zester or a very fine grater, simply grate the outside peel of the fruit.

2 pounds (910 g) firm, ripe pears*

1¾ cups (414 ml) water

1 tablespoon (5 g) zest from a lemon

1 teaspoon (2 g) ground cardamom

½ cup (120 ml) lemon juice

2 teaspoons (10 ml) calcium water**

1 cup (200 g) sugar

1½ teaspoons (4.5 g) Pomona's pectin powder

*Not sure how much fruit to purchase? See "Measuring Up!" on page 26.

**For information on how to prepare calcium water, refer to page 22.

1. If you are new to canning, or need a refresher, refer to chapter 1 (pages 12–41) for step-by-step guidance and additional information on how to safely can your preserves. Once ready, proceed as follows.
2. Prepare your jars, lids, and bands; heat up your canner; and sterilize your jars.
3. Peel and core pears. Quarter them lengthwise, and then slice each quarter into a couple of smaller, uniform, lengthwise slices.
4. Combine sliced pears and 1¾ cups (414 ml) water in a saucepan. Bring to a boil over high heat, reduce heat, and simmer, covered, for 3 to 5 minutes until fruit is soft (but still retains its shape), stirring occasionally. Remove from heat.
5. Measure 4 cups (946 ml) of the cooked pears (saving any extra for another use), and return the measured quantity to the saucepan. Add lemon zest, cardamom, lemon juice, and calcium water. Mix well.
6. In a separate bowl, combine sugar and pectin powder. Mix thoroughly and set aside.
7. Bring pear mixture to a full boil over high heat. Slowly add pectin-sugar mixture, stirring constantly. Continue to stir vigorously for 1 to 2 minutes to dissolve pectin while the preserves come back up to a boil. Once the preserves return to a full boil, remove the pan from the heat.
8. **Can Your Preserves:** Remove jars from canner and ladle hot preserves into hot jars, leaving ¼ inch (6 mm) of headspace. Remove trapped air bubbles, wipe rims with a damp cloth, put on lids and screw bands, and tighten to fingertip tight. Lower filled jars into canner, ensuring jars are not touching each other and are covered with at least 1 to 2 inches (2.5 to 5 cm) of water. Place lid on canner, return to a rolling boil, and process for 10 minutes (adjusting for altitude if necessary). Turn off heat and allow canner to sit untouched for 5 minutes, then remove jars and allow to cool undisturbed for 12 to 24 hours. Confirm that jars have sealed, then store properly.

YIELD: 4 TO 5 HALF-PINT (8-OUNCE, OR 236 ML) JARS

FRESH AND FIRM

For this recipe, be sure to use pears that are still quite firm, so the pear slices remain intact when cooked.

BRANDIED CINNAMON-APPLE PRESERVES

Featuring apple slices in a sweet, spiced, brandy-infused jelled syrup, this preserve is extremely versatile. It's wonderful with butter on toast, of course, but it's equally at home as a topping on a tart or as filling in a crisp (served with ice cream, naturally!). Be sure to use crisp, hard apples for this preserve, so that the fruit retains a bit of its shape when cooked.

||||||||||||||||||||||||||||||||||||||||||||||||||||||||||||||||||||||||||||||||||||||||||||||||||||||||||||||||||||||||||||||||||||||||

2 pounds (910 g) crisp, hard apples*

1¾ cups (414 ml) water

1 teaspoon (2.3 g) cinnamon

½ cup (120 ml) brandy

¼ cup (60 ml) lemon juice

2 teaspoons (10 ml) calcium water**

1 cup (200 g) sugar

1½ teaspoons (4.5 g) Pomona's pectin powder

*Not sure how much fruit to purchase? See "Measuring Up!" on page 26.

**For information on how to prepare calcium water, refer to page 22.

1. If you are new to canning, or need a refresher, refer to chapter 1 (pages 12–41) for step-by-step guidance and additional information on how to safely can your preserves. Once ready, proceed as follows.
2. Prepare your jars, lids, and bands; heat up your canner; and sterilize your jars.
3. Peel apples, remove stems and cores, and quarter them. Then slice each quarter into a few smaller, uniform, lengthwise slices.
4. Combine sliced apples and the 1¾ cups (414 ml) water in a saucepan. Bring to a boil over high heat, reduce heat, and simmer, covered, for 3 to 5 minutes, until fruit is soft (but still retains its shape), stirring occasionally. Remove from heat.
5. Measure 4 cups (946 ml) of the cooked apples (saving any extra for another use), and return the measured quantity to the saucepan. Add cinnamon, brandy, lemon juice, and calcium water. Mix well.
6. In a separate bowl, combine sugar and pectin powder. Mix thoroughly and set aside.
7. Bring apple mixture to a full boil over high heat. Slowly add pectin-sugar mixture, stirring constantly. Continue to stir vigorously for 1 to 2 minutes to dissolve pectin while the preserves come back up to a boil. Once the preserves return to a full boil, remove the pan from the heat.
8. **Can Your Preserves:** Remove jars from canner and ladle hot preserves into hot jars, leaving ¼ inch (6 mm) of headspace. Remove trapped air bubbles, wipe rims with a damp cloth, put on lids and screw bands, and tighten to fingertip tight. Lower filled jars into canner, ensuring jars are not touching each other and are covered with at least 1 to 2 inches (2.5 to 5 cm) of water. Place lid on canner, return to a rolling boil, and process for 10 minutes (adjusting for altitude if necessary). Turn off heat and allow canner to sit untouched for 5 minutes, then remove jars and allow to cool undisturbed for 12 to 24 hours. Confirm that jars have sealed, then store properly.

YIELD: 4 TO 5 HALF-PINT (8-OUNCE, OR 236 ML) JARS

||||||||||||||||||||||||||||||||||||||||||||||||||||||||||||||||||||||||||||

CUSTOMIZE IT!

If you prefer a less-processed sugar, such as turbinado (raw sugar), you can use that instead of regular white sugar. Just be sure to pulse it in a food processor a few times to make the granules fine enough that you'll be able to mix the pectin into the sugar effectively.

||||||||||||||||||||||||||||||||||||||||||||||||||||||||||||||||||||||||||||

MANGO-GINGER PRESERVES

Mango and ginger is a common pairing in many Asian cuisines, and it makes sense—the unique heat and bite of ginger is a perfect counterpoint to the intense, sultry sweetness of a ripe mango. This recipe calls for crystallized ginger, a convenient alternative to fresh ginger, available at Asian markets and natural food stores. While mangoes should be ripe, be sure to use ones that are still firm, so that they hold their shape in this preserve.

||||||||||||||||||||||||||||||||||||||||||||||||||||||||||||||||||||||||||||||||||||||||||||||||||||||||

3½ pounds (1.6 kg) firm, ripe mangoes*

2 tablespoons (28 g) finely chopped crystallized ginger

½ cup (120 ml) lemon juice, divided

4 teaspoons (20 ml) calcium water**

1¼ cups (250 g) sugar

3 teaspoons (9 g) Pomona's pectin powder

*Not sure how much fruit to purchase? See "Measuring Up!" on page 26.

**For information on how to prepare calcium water, refer to page 22.

||||||||||||||||||||||||||||||||||||||||||||||||||||||||||||||||||||||

EVEN IT OUT!

Hot preserves that have not yet jelled have distinct solids (the fruit) and liquids (the syrup, which has not yet jelled). Because of this, when filling jars, it's easy to inadvertently put all the fruit in just a few of the jars, leaving a lot of extra fruit-less liquid. To avoid this, fill each jar with both solids and liquids, aiming for roughly the same amount of solids in each jar. Once you have all the jars filled, before putting the lids on, carefully move fruit and liquid in and out of jars as necessary, using a teaspoon, to even things out.

1. If you are new to canning, or need a refresher, refer to chapter 1 (pages 12–41) for step-by-step guidance and additional information on how to safely can your preserves. Once ready, proceed as follows.
2. Prepare your jars, lids, and bands; heat up your canner; and sterilize your jars.
3. Peel, pit, and dice mangoes into uniform-size cubes (for more information, see "Mango Madness!" on page 63).
4. Combine mangoes in a saucepan with crystallized ginger and ¼ cup (60 ml) of the lemon juice. Bring to a boil over high heat, reduce heat, and simmer, covered, for 3 to 5 minutes until fruit is soft (but still retains its shape), stirring occasionally. Remove from heat.
5. Measure 4 cups (946 ml) of the cooked mango mixture (saving any extra for another use), and return the measured quantity to the saucepan. Add the remaining ¼ cup (60 ml) of lemon juice, and the calcium water. Mix well.
6. In a separate bowl, combine sugar and pectin powder. Mix thoroughly and set aside.
7. Bring mango mixture back to a full boil over high heat. Slowly add pectin-sugar mixture, stirring constantly. Continue to stir vigorously for 1 to 2 minutes to dissolve pectin while the preserves come back up to a boil. Once the preserves return to a full boil, remove the pan from the heat.
8. **Can Your Preserves:** Remove jars from canner and ladle hot preserves into hot jars, leaving ¼ inch (6 mm) of headspace. Remove trapped air bubbles, wipe rims with a damp cloth, put on lids and screw bands, and tighten to fingertip tight. Lower filled jars into canner, ensuring jars are not touching each other and are covered with at least 1 to 2 inches (2.5 to 5 cm) of water. Place lid on canner, return to a rolling boil, and process for 10 minutes (adjusting for altitude if necessary). Turn off heat and allow canner to sit untouched for 5 minutes, then remove jars and allow to cool undisturbed for 12 to 24 hours. Confirm that jars have sealed, then store properly.

YIELD: 4 TO 5 HALF-PINT (8-OUNCE, OR 236 ML) JARS

||||||||||||||||||||||||||||||||||||||||||||||||||||||||

SPICED GRAPE PRESERVES

Most of us are so accustomed to grapes being made into jelly that it's easy to forget that they can be put up in many other ways. This lightly spiced, dark purple preserve is a delightfully different way to enjoy grapes. It's a perfect, just-sweet-enough topping for yogurt and granola in a big bowl for breakfast.

IIIIIIIIIIIIIIIIIIIIIIIIIIIIIIIIIIIIIIIIIIIIIIIIIIIIIIIIIIIIIIIIIIIIIIIIIIIIIIIIIIIIIIIIIIIIIIIIIIIIIIIIIIIIIIIIIIIIIIIIIIIIIIII

2½ pounds (1.1 kg) sweet, seedless, purple or black grapes*

¼ cup (60 ml) orange juice

½ teaspoon (1.25 g) ground cinnamon

¼ teaspoon (0.75 g) ground cloves

¼ teaspoon (0.7 g) ground ginger

¼ cup (60 ml) lemon juice

4 teaspoons (20 ml) calcium water**

¾ cup (150 g) sugar

3 teaspoons (9 g) Pomona's pectin powder

*Not sure how much fruit to purchase? See "Measuring Up!" on page 26.

**For information on how to prepare calcium water, refer to page 22.

1. If you are new to canning, or need a refresher, refer to chapter 1 (pages 12–41) for step-by-step guidance and additional information on how to safely can your preserves. Once ready, proceed as follows.
2. Prepare your jars, lids, and bands; heat up your canner; and sterilize your jars.
3. Rinse grapes, remove stems, and slice grapes in half.
4. Combine grapes with orange juice in a saucepan. Bring to a boil over high heat, reduce heat, and simmer, covered, for 7 to 10 minutes or until fruit is soft, stirring occasionally. Remove from heat.
5. Measure 4 cups (946 ml) of the cooked mixture (saving any extra for another use), and return the measured quantity to the saucepan. Add cinnamon, cloves, ground ginger, lemon juice, and calcium water. Mix well.
6. In a separate bowl, combine sugar and pectin powder. Mix thoroughly and set aside.
7. Bring grape mixture back to a full boil over high heat. Slowly add pectin-sugar mixture, stirring constantly. Continue to stir vigorously for 1 to 2 minutes to dissolve pectin while the preserves come back up to a boil. Once the preserves return to a full boil, remove the pan from the heat.
8. **Can Your Preserves:** Remove jars from canner and ladle hot preserves into hot jars, leaving ¼ inch (6 mm) of headspace. Remove trapped air bubbles, wipe rims with a damp cloth, put on lids and screw bands, and tighten to fingertip tight. Lower filled jars into canner, ensuring jars are not touching each other and are covered with at least 1 to 2 inches (2.5 to 5 cm) of water. Place lid on canner, return to a rolling boil, and process for 10 minutes (adjusting for altitude if necessary). Turn off heat and allow canner to sit untouched for 5 minutes, then remove jars and allow to cool undisturbed for 12 to 24 hours. Confirm that jars have sealed, then store properly.

YIELD: 4 TO 5 HALF-PINT (8-OUNCE, OR 236 ML) JARS

IIIIIIIIIIIIIIIIIIIIIIIIIIIIIIIIIIIIIIIIIIIIIIIIIIIIIIIIIII

CUSTOMIZE IT!

If you're looking for something new, why not try honey instead of sugar? In place of the sugar in this recipe, use ½ to 1 cup (170 to 340 g) honey.

IIIIIIIIIIIIIIIIIIIIIIIIIIIIIIIIIIIIIIIIIIIIIIIIIIII

BRANDIED APRICOT PRESERVES with LEMON PEEL

This preserve is both delicious and visually stunning, with thin strips of lemon peel suspended among lovely, orange fruit pieces. For a gorgeous, eye-catching dessert, spread it on top of plain cheesecake. This preserve also makes a wonderful gift.

2 pounds (910 g) ripe apricots*

3 medium lemons, divided

¾ cup (175 ml) brandy

⅛ cup (30 ml) water

3½ teaspoons (17.5 ml) calcium water**

1¼ cups (250 g) sugar

2½ teaspoons (7.5 g) Pomona's pectin powder

*Not sure how much fruit to purchase? See "Measuring Up!" on page 26.

**For information on how to prepare your calcium water, refer to page 24.

1. If you are new to canning, or need a refresher, refer to chapter 1 (pages 12–41) for step-by-step guidance and additional information on how to safely can your preserves. Once ready, proceed as follows.
2. Prepare your jars, lids, and bands; heat up your canner; and sterilize your jars.
3. Rinse apricots, remove stems, and then slice in half or pull apart. Remove pits, cut apricots into uniform pieces, and set them aside. (For more information, see "To Peel or Not to Peel?" on page 76.)
4. Wash lemons thoroughly. Using a vegetable peeler, slice off long pieces of the exterior of some of the lemon peels, avoiding the inner white part. Then, using a chef's knife, slice these pieces into very thin strips about 1-inch (2.5 cm) long. Repeat this process until you have accumulated ¼ cup (24 g) of thin strips.
5. Combine apricot pieces and the ¼ cup (24 g) lemon strips in a saucepan with brandy and the ⅛ cup (30 ml) water.
6. Slice the 3 lemons in half and squeeze out their juice, discarding the remaining peels. Divide the juice, setting aside ⅓ cup (75 ml) for later use. Add the remaining quantity to the apricot mixture.
7. Bring apricot mixture to a boil over high heat, reduce heat, and simmer, covered, for 12 to 15 minutes or until lemon peels are soft. Remove from heat.
8. Measure 4 cups (946 ml) of the apricot mixture, and return the measured quantity to the saucepan. Add the reserved ⅓ cup (75 ml) lemon juice and calcium water, and mix well.
9. In a separate bowl, combine sugar and pectin powder. Mix thoroughly and set aside.
10. Bring fruit back to a full boil over high heat. Slowly add pectin-sugar mixture, stirring constantly. Continue to stir vigorously for 1 to 2 minutes to dissolve pectin while the preserves come back up to a boil. Once the mixture returns to a full boil, remove it from the heat.
11. **Can Your Preserves:** Remove jars from canner and ladle hot preserves into hot jars, leaving ¼ inch (6 mm) of headspace. Remove trapped air bubbles, wipe rims with a damp cloth, put on lids and screw bands, and tighten to fingertip tight. Lower filled jars into canner, ensuring jars are not touching each other and are covered with at least 1 to 2 inches (2.5 to 5 cm) of water. Place lid on canner, return to a rolling boil, and process for 10 minutes (adjusting for altitude if necessary). Turn off heat and allow canner to sit untouched for 5 minutes, then remove jars and allow to cool undisturbed for 12 to 24 hours. Confirm that jars have sealed, then store properly.

YIELD: 4 TO 5 HALF-PINT (8-OUNCE, OR 236 ML) JARS

DOUBLE UP!

If you're making a favorite recipe, why not make a double batch? Unlike with other pectins, a double (or even triple) batch is no problem with Pomona's. Simply do the math, doubling everything—and don't forget the extra jars!

STRAWBERRY-VANILLA PRESERVES

With ripe in-season strawberries, combined with a smooth, exotic note of fresh vanilla, this preserve is nothing short of heavenly. It will add a bit of flair to the breakfast table (or bagel) of course, but it's also great in desserts—try it on top of a biscuit with a bit of whipped cream for a spectacular strawberry-vanilla shortcake! The berries in this preserve tend to float to the top during canning, so mix it up well before serving.

IIIIIIIIIIIIIIIIIIIIIIIIIIIIIIIIIIIIIIIIIIIIIIIIIIIIIIIIIIIIIIIIIIIIIIIIIIIIIIIIIIIIIIIIIIIIIIIIIIIIIIIIIIIIIIIIIIIIIIIIIIIIIIIIIIIIIIIIIIIIIIIIIIIIIIIIII

2¼ pounds (1 kg) strawberries*

½ cup (120 ml) water

1 vanilla bean

1½ teaspoons (7.5 g) calcium water**

1¼ cups (250 g) sugar

1½ teaspoons (4.5 g) Pomona's pectin powder

Not sure how much fruit to purchase? See "Measuring Up!" on page 26.

***For information on how to prepare calcium water, refer to page 22.*

1. If you are new to canning, or need a refresher, refer to chapter 1 (pages 12–41) for step-by-step guidance and additional information on how to safely can your preserves. Once ready, proceed as follows.
2. Prepare your jars, lids, and bands; heat up your canner; and sterilize your jars.
3. Rinse strawberries and remove stems.
4. Combine strawberries and the ½ cup (120 ml) of water in a large saucepan. Using a paring knife, slice the vanilla bean in half lengthwise and scrape out the seeds. Add the vanilla seeds and the bean pod itself to the strawberries. Bring the mixture to a boil over high heat, reduce heat, and simmer, covered, for 3 to 4 minutes, stirring occasionally. Stir carefully—you don't want to crush the berries. Remove from heat.
5. Measure 4 cups (946 ml) of the cooked strawberry mixture (saving any extra for another use), and return the measured quantity to the saucepan. Add calcium water and mix well.
6. In a separate bowl, combine sugar and pectin powder. Mix thoroughly and set aside.
7. Bring strawberry mixture back to a full boil over high heat. Slowly add pectin-sugar mixture, stirring constantly. Continue to stir vigorously for 1 to 2 minutes to dissolve pectin while the preserves come back up to a boil. Once the preserves return to a full boil, remove the pan from the heat. Using tongs, carefully remove the vanilla bean pod from the preserves and discard.
8. **Can Your Preserves:** Remove jars from canner and ladle hot preserves into hot jars, leaving ¼ inch (6 mm) of headspace. Remove trapped air bubbles, wipe rims with a damp cloth, put on lids and screw bands, and tighten to fingertip tight. Lower filled jars into canner, ensuring jars are not touching each other and are covered with at least 1 to 2 inches (2.5 to 5 cm) of water. Place lid on canner, return to a rolling boil, and process for 10 minutes (adjusting for altitude if necessary). Turn off heat and allow canner to sit untouched for 5 minutes, then remove jars and allow to cool undisturbed for 12 to 24 hours. Confirm that jars have sealed, then store properly.

YIELD: 4 TO 5 HALF-PINT (8-OUNCE, OR 236 ML) JARS

SHAPELY STRAWBERRIES

Unlike jams, which usually require that you mash the fruit, when you're making preserves, the idea is to keep individual pieces of fruit (or uniformly cut pieces of fruit) mostly whole and intact. For strawberries, small or average-size berries are ideal, though larger berries will work—simply slice them in half if they are too big. To help avoid mashing delicate fruit unintentionally, use a wider saucepan so that fruit has room to spread out and cook evenly without a lot of stirring. And when you do stir, stir with a back-and-forth motion, rather than an up-and-down motion—this way you'll be less likely to crush the berries.

GINGERED LEMON-FIG PRESERVES

In this spectacular preserve, a touch of heat from the ginger and a little tartness from the lemons beautifully highlight the lushness of fresh, ripe figs. Try serving sandwiched between gingersnap cookies to accentuate its flavor profile. To ensure proper acidity levels, be sure to use commonly available, full-acid lemons such as Eureka or Lisbon lemons in this recipe.

|||||||||||||||||||||||||||||||||||||||||||||||||||||||||||||||||||||||||||||||||||||||||||||||||||||||||||||||||||||||||||||||||||||||||||||||||||||||||||||||||||||||

2 pounds (910 g) ripe figs*

2 tablespoons peeled, finely grated ginger root

7 medium lemons, divided

4 teaspoons (20 ml) calcium water**

1¼ cups (250 g) sugar

3 teaspoons (9 g) Pomona's pectin powder

*Not sure how much fruit to purchase? See "Measuring Up!" on page 26.

**For information on how to prepare calcium water, refer to page 22.

|||||||||||||||||||||||||||||||||||||||||||||||||||||||||||||||||||

GRATE THAT GINGER!

Using a paring knife or a vegetable peeler, slice the thin, brown skin off a chunk of fresh, firm ginger root. Then, using a fine mesh grater, grate the ginger root. Don't peel the whole root at once—continue to peel as you go along, so that you don't peel more than you need. Grating the ginger will create a good bit of juice; be sure to incorporate it into your measured quantity of grated ginger.

1. If you are new to canning, or need a refresher, refer to chapter 1 (pages 12–41) for step-by-step guidance and additional information on how to safely can your preserves. Once ready, proceed as follows.
2. Prepare your jars, lids, and bands; heat up your canner; and sterilize your jars.
3. Rinse figs, remove stems, and slice them in half lengthwise. (Cut them into smaller pieces if you prefer, or if you're working with large figs.) Combine figs in a saucepan with grated ginger.
4. Wash lemons thoroughly. Using a vegetable peeler, slice off long pieces of the exterior of some of the lemon peels, avoiding the inner white part. Then, using a chef's knife, slice these pieces into very thin strips about 1-inch (2.5 cm) long. Repeat this process until you have accumulated ¼ cup of thin, 1-inch (2.5 cm) long strips. Add these strips to the fig mixture.
5. Slice lemons in half and squeeze out their juice, discarding the remaining peels. Divide the juice, setting aside ⅓ cup (75 ml) for later use. Add the remaining quantity to the fig mixture.
6. Bring the fig mixture to a boil over high heat, reduce heat, and simmer, covered, for 12 to 15 minutes or until lemon peels are soft, stirring occasionally. Remove from heat.
7. Measure 4 cups (946 ml) of the cooked fig mixture and return the measured quantity to the saucepan. Add the reserved ⅓ cup (75 ml) lemon juice and calcium water and mix well.
8. In a separate bowl, combine sugar and pectin powder. Mix thoroughly and set aside.
9. Bring fig mixture back to a full boil over high heat. Slowly add pectin-sugar mixture, stirring constantly. Continue to stir vigorously for 1 to 2 minutes to dissolve pectin while the preserves come back up to a boil. Once the preserves return to a full boil, remove from heat.
10. **Can Your Preserves:** Remove jars from canner and ladle hot preserves into hot jars, leaving ¼ inch (6 mm) of headspace. Remove trapped air bubbles, wipe rims with a damp cloth, put on lids and screw bands, and tighten to fingertip tight. Lower filled jars into canner, ensuring jars are not touching each other and are covered with at least 1 to 2 inches (2.5 to 5 cm) of water. Place lid on canner, return to a rolling boil, and process for 10 minutes (adjusting for altitude if necessary). Turn off heat and allow canner to sit untouched for 5 minutes, then remove jars and allow to cool undisturbed for 12 to 24 hours. Confirm that jars have sealed, then store properly.

YIELD: 4 TO 5 HALF-PINT (8-OUNCE, OR 236 ML) JARS

|||||||||||||||||||||||||||||||||||||||||||||||||||||||||||||||||||

CHOCOLATE-CHERRY PRESERVES

Chocolate and cherries were made for each other, and this preserve is proof. The combination of the two is insanely decadent. Be sure to use high-quality cocoa powder that is unsweetened and has no other added ingredients. Spoon this preserve on top of cheesecake for a stunning—and absolutely heavenly—dessert.

2½ pounds (1.1 kg) sweet cherries*

⅓ cup (29 g) sifted, unsweetened cocoa powder

½ cup (120 ml) water

¼ teaspoon (0.6 g) cinnamon

⅛ teaspoon (0.25 g) cayenne pepper

¼ cup (60 ml) lemon juice

3 teaspoons (15 ml) calcium water**

1¼ cups (250 g) sugar

2½ teaspoons (7.5 g) Pomona's pectin powder

*Not sure how much fruit to purchase? See "Measuring Up!" on page 26.

**For information on how to prepare calcium water, refer to page 22.

1. If you are new to canning, or need a refresher, refer to chapter 1 (pages 12–41) for step-by-step guidance and additional information on how to safely can your preserves. Once ready, proceed as follows.
2. Prepare your jars, lids, and bands; heat up your canner; and sterilize your jars.
3. Rinse cherries, remove stems, and then slice in half and remove pits. (For more information, see "Painless Pitting" on page 70.)
4. Combine cherry halves with cocoa powder and the ½ cup (120 ml) of water in a saucepan. Bring to a boil over high heat, reduce heat, and simmer, covered, for 5 minutes, stirring occasionally. Remove from heat.
5. Measure 4 cups (946 ml) of the cooked mixture (saving any extra for another use), and return the measured quantity to the saucepan. Add cinnamon, cayenne pepper, lemon juice, and calcium water. Mix well.
6. In a separate bowl, combine sugar and pectin powder. Mix thoroughly and set aside.
7. Bring cherry mixture back to a full boil over high heat. Slowly add pectin-sugar mixture, stirring constantly. Continue to stir vigorously for 1 to 2 minutes to dissolve pectin while the preserves come back up to a boil. Once the mixture returns to a full boil, remove the pan from the heat.
8. **Can Your Preserves:** Remove jars from canner and ladle hot preserves into hot jars, leaving ¼ inch (6 mm) of headspace. Remove trapped air bubbles, wipe rims with a damp cloth, put on lids and screw bands, and tighten to fingertip tight. Lower filled jars into canner, ensuring jars are not touching each other and are covered with at least 1 to 2 inches (2.5 to 5 cm) of water. Place lid on canner, return to a rolling boil, and process for 10 minutes (adjusting for altitude if necessary). Turn off heat and allow canner to sit untouched for 5 minutes, then remove jars and allow to cool undisturbed for 12 to 24 hours. Confirm that jars have sealed, then store properly.

YIELD: 4 TO 5 HALF-PINT (8-OUNCE, OR 236 ML) JARS

Chapter 5

CONSERVES

By definition, conserves contain an assortment of different ingredients, so they are much more varied than any of the other jelled goods. In addition to the primary fruit, conserves are studded with a variety of other ingredients, such as dried fruit, nuts, or vegetables, and they can be either sweet or savory. In their sweet form, conserves are similar to jams, but usually with an added dose of chewy or crunchy texture. Savory conserves are often deliciously unexpected. With the inclusion of onions, ginger, garlic, and other earthy spices, they are excellent as glazes on roasted or grilled meats and vegetables, or as a condiment. This chapter contains a variety of conserves, both savory and sweet, so prepare yourself to enjoy some delicious—and perhaps unexpected—flavor combinations!

PEACH-PECAN-CHERRY CONSERVE

This luscious conserve makes me think of my maternal grandmother and her simple, self-sufficient life in rural Georgia. She and her neighbor shared the bounty of a beautiful old pecan tree, and after my grandmother died, her neighbor would mail a package of pecans picked from that tree to my mother every Christmas. These are the pecans I used when I created this recipe. Select peaches that are still somewhat firm so that the fruit will retain its shape when cooked.

2 pounds (910 g) ripe, firm peaches*

⅔ cup (100 g) dried cherries

½ cup (55 g) chopped pecans

1 cup (235 ml) water

¼ cup (60 ml) lemon juice

4 teaspoons (20 ml) calcium water**

¾ cup (150 g) sugar

3 teaspoons (9 g) Pomona's pectin powder

*Not sure how much fruit to purchase? See "Measuring Up!" on page 26.

**For information on how to prepare calcium water, refer to page 22.

1. If you are new to canning, or need a refresher, refer to chapter 1 (pages 12–41) for step-by-step guidance and additional information on how to safely can your conserve. Once ready, proceed as follows.
2. Prepare your jars, lids, and bands; heat up your canner; and sterilize your jars.
3. Peel, remove pits, and dice peaches. (For more information, see "How to Skin a Peach" on page 58.)
4. Combine diced peaches in a saucepan with dried cherries, chopped pecans, and the 1 cup (235 ml) water. Bring to a boil over high heat, reduce heat, and simmer, covered, for 5 to 10 minutes, or until fruit is soft, stirring occasionally. Remove from heat.
5. Measure 4 cups (946 ml) of the cooked mixture (saving any extra for another use), and return the measured quantity to the saucepan. Add the lemon juice and calcium water, and mix well.
6. In a separate bowl, combine sugar and pectin powder. Mix thoroughly and set aside.
7. Bring peach mixture back to a full boil over high heat. Slowly add pectin-sugar mixture, stirring constantly. Continue to stir vigorously for 1 to 2 minutes to dissolve pectin while the conserve comes back up to a boil. Once the conserve returns to a full boil, remove it from the heat.
8. **Can Your Conserve:** Remove jars from canner and ladle hot conserve into hot jars, leaving ¼ inch (6 mm) of headspace. Remove trapped air bubbles, wipe rims with a damp cloth, put on lids and screw bands, and tighten to fingertip tight. Lower filled jars into canner, ensuring jars are not touching each other and are covered with at least 1 to 2 inches (2.5 to 5 cm) of water. Place lid on canner, return to a rolling boil, and process for 10 minutes (adjusting for altitude if necessary). Turn off heat and allow canner to sit untouched for 5 minutes, then remove jars and allow to cool undisturbed for 12 to 24 hours. Confirm that jars have sealed, then store properly.

YIELD: 4 TO 5 HALF-PINT (8-OUNCE, OR 236 ML) JARS

CUSTOMIZE IT!

Looking for something new? Try using lime juice in place of the lemon juice in this recipe.

PEAR-CRANBERRY CONSERVE with ALMONDS AND CRYSTALLIZED GINGER

The combination of pear and cranberry is a delightful one for fall. The addition of ginger really makes the flavors sing, and the almonds provide a chewy crunch. For the best texture, use pears that are still quite firm so that the pear pieces remain intact when cooked. While unsweetened dried fruit is generally preferable in conserves, it's very difficult to find unsweetened dried cranberries, so feel free to use the sweetened version if that's what you have available.

2 pounds (910 g) ripe, firm pears*

½ cup (75 g) dried cranberries

2 tablespoons (28 g) finely chopped crystallized ginger

½ cup (63 g) sliced almonds

1½ cups (355 ml) water

½ cup (120 ml) lemon juice

4 teaspoons (20 ml) calcium water**

1 cup (200 g) sugar

3 teaspoons (9 g) Pomona's pectin powder

*Not sure how much fruit to purchase? See "Measuring Up!" on page 26.

**For information on how to prepare calcium water, refer to page 22.

1. If you are new to canning, or need a refresher, refer to chapter 1 (pages 12–41) for step-by-step guidance and additional information on how to safely can your conserve. Once ready, proceed as follows.
2. Prepare your jars, lids, and bands; heat up your canner; and sterilize your jars.
3. Peel, core, and dice pears.
4. Combine diced pears in a saucepan with dried cranberries, crystallized ginger, sliced almonds, and the 1½ cups (355 ml) water. Bring to a boil over high heat, reduce heat, and simmer, covered, for 5 to 10 minutes or until fruit is soft, stirring occasionally. Remove from heat. Mix well.
5. Measure 4 cups (946 ml) of the cooked mixture (saving any extra for another use), and return the measured quantity to the saucepan. Add lemon juice and calcium water, and mix well.
6. In a separate bowl, combine sugar and pectin powder. Mix thoroughly and set aside.
7. Bring pear mixture back to a full boil over high heat. Slowly add the pectin-sugar mixture, stirring constantly. Continue to stir vigorously for 1 to 2 minutes to dissolve pectin while the conserve comes back up to a boil. Once the conserve returns to a full boil, remove it from the heat.
8. **Can Your Conserve:** Remove jars from canner and ladle hot conserve into hot jars, leaving ¼ inch (6 mm) of headspace. Remove trapped air bubbles, wipe rims with a damp cloth, put on lids and screw bands, and tighten to fingertip tight. Lower filled jars into canner, ensuring jars are not touching each other and are covered with at least 1 to 2 inches (2.5 to 5 cm) of water. Place lid on canner, return to a rolling boil, and process for 10 minutes (adjusting for altitude if necessary). Turn off heat and allow canner to sit untouched for 5 minutes, then remove jars and allow to cool undisturbed for 12 to 24 hours. Confirm that jars have sealed, then store properly.

YIELD: 4 TO 5 HALF-PINT (8-OUNCE, OR 236 ML) JARS

CRYSTALLIZE IT!

This recipe calls for crystallized ginger—essentially, slices of fresh ginger root that have been cooked and preserved with sugar. Crystallized ginger is easy and quick to chop, so it's very convenient in recipes. It's available at Asian markets and at many natural food stores.

PERSNICKETY PINEAPPLES!

With such a tough, prickly exterior, the prospect of cutting up a whole pineapple can be daunting. Fortunately, if you follow a few simple steps, it's easy to do. Start by laying the pineapple on its side on a cutting board, and, using a chef's knife, slice off the top end of the pineapple (the part with the green leaves) and the base of the pineapple. Then stand the pineapple upright and slice vertically down the side of the pineapple, slicing off one section of the skin. Rotate the pineapple slightly and slice off the next section of skin in the same manner. Work your way all the way around the pineapple until you've sliced off all the tough exterior. Use a small melon baller or a paring knife to remove any remaining bits of the tough exterior embedded in the flesh. Stand the pineapple upright and, looking at the top of the pineapple, locate the white core, which runs lengthwise through the middle of the fruit. With the pineapple still upright, slice vertically down the edge of the core, slicing the flesh off the core. Rotate the pineapple and slice off the next section of flesh in the same manner, until you've sliced all of the flesh off the core. Discard the core, and cut up the pineapple flesh as called for in your recipe.

GOLDEN PINEAPPLE-CRANBERRY CONSERVE

This gorgeous, bright-red conserve is a wonderful combination of the tartness of cranberries and the intense, lush sweetness of fresh pineapple. Raisins contribute sweetness as well. I use golden ones, as their color is especially suitable for this conserve, but you can go with dark raisins if you like. Whole cranberries give this conserve a pleasing texture, but if you prefer your cranberries chopped up, feel free to give them a whirl in your food processor before cooking them.

1 bag (12 ounces, or 340 g) cranberries

2 cups (330 g) chopped pineapple*

¾ cup (109 g) golden raisins (or dark raisins, if you prefer)

1¼ cups (296 ml) water

2 tablespoons (30 ml) lemon juice

2 teaspoons (10 ml) calcium water*

1½ cups (300 g) sugar

2 teaspoons (6 g) Pomona's pectin powder

*Not sure how much fruit to purchase? See "Measuring Up!" on page 26.

**For information on how to prepare calcium water, refer to page 22.

1. If you are new to canning, or need a refresher, refer to chapter 1 (pages 12–41) for step-by-step guidance and additional information on how to safely can your conserve. Once ready, proceed as follows.

2. Prepare your jars, lids, and bands; heat up your canner; and sterilize your jars.

3. Rinse cranberries and combine in a saucepan with pineapple, raisins, and the 1¼ cups (296 ml) water. Bring fruit mixture to a boil over high heat, reduce heat, and simmer for 10 minutes, or until fruit is soft and most cranberries have burst, stirring occasionally. Remove from heat.

4. Measure 4 cups (946 ml) of the cooked fruit mixture (saving any extra for another use), and return the measured quantity to the saucepan. Add lemon juice and calcium water, and mix well.

5. In a separate bowl, combine sugar and pectin powder. Mix thoroughly and set aside.

6. Bring fruit mixture back to a full boil over high heat. Slowly add pectin-sugar mixture, stirring constantly. Continue to stir vigorously for 1 to 2 minutes to dissolve pectin while the conserve comes back up to a boil. Once the conserve returns to a full boil, remove it from the heat.

7. **Can Your Conserve:** Remove jars from canner and ladle hot conserve into hot jars, leaving ¼ inch (6 mm) of headspace. Remove trapped air bubbles, wipe rims with a damp cloth, put on lids and screw bands, and tighten to fingertip tight. Lower filled jars into canner, ensuring jars are not touching each other and are covered with at least 1 to 2 inches (2.5 to 5 cm) of water. Place lid on canner, return to a rolling boil, and process for 10 minutes (adjusting for altitude if necessary). Turn off heat and allow canner to sit untouched for 5 minutes, then remove jars and allow to cool undisturbed for 12 to 24 hours. Confirm that jars have sealed, then store properly.

YIELD: 4 TO 5 HALF-PINT (8-OUNCE, OR 236 ML) JARS

SAVORY BLUEBERRY-GINGER CONSERVE

If you're looking for an alternative to cranberry sauce on your holiday table this fall and winter, give this gorgeous, savory conserve a try. With fresh ginger, orange peel, and other warm and earthy spices, it is a delicious, unexpected accompaniment to roasted meats and vegetables—and of course the lunches you make with the leftovers! Remember, for canning safety, don't increase the quantity of vegetables or spices, and be sure to use bottled lemon juice.

1½ pounds (680 g) blueberries*

¾ cup (120 g) diced onion

2 tablespoons (28 g) peeled, finely grated ginger root (for more information, see "Grate That Ginger!" on page 125)

¾ cup (175 ml) white vinegar

1 teaspoon (3.7 g) mustard seed

¼ teaspoon (0.6 g) ground cinnamon

¼ teaspoon (0.75 g) ground cloves

¼ teaspoon (0.5 g) ground cardamom

½ teaspoon (0.85 g) ground black pepper

½ teaspoon (3 g) salt

2 medium oranges

2 tablespoons (30 ml) lemon juice

2 teaspoons (10 ml) calcium water**

1 cup (200 g) sugar

2 teaspoons (6 g) Pomona's pectin powder

*Not sure how much fruit to purchase? See "Measuring Up!" on page 26.

**For information on how to prepare calcium water, refer to page 22.

1. If you are new to canning, or need a refresher, refer to chapter 1 (pages 12–41) for step-by-step guidance and additional information on how to safely can your conserve. Once ready, proceed as follows.
2. Prepare your jars, lids, and bands; heat up your canner; and sterilize your jars.
3. Rinse the blueberries, remove stems, and combine in a large saucepan with onion, ginger, vinegar, mustard seed, cinnamon, cloves, cardamom, black pepper, and salt.
4. Wash oranges thoroughly. Using a vegetable peeler, peel off some of the outer part of the orange peels, avoiding the inner white part, and chop finely. Repeat this process until you have accumulated 2 tablespoons (12 g) of finely chopped orange peel. Then, slice the oranges in half and squeeze out their juice. Add the 2 tablespoons (12 g) orange peel and the orange juice to the blueberry mixture, and discard the remaining peels.
5. Bring blueberry mixture to a boil over high heat, reduce heat, and simmer, covered, for 15 minutes, stirring occasionally. Remove from heat.
6. Measure 4 cups (946 ml) of the cooked blueberry mixture (saving any extra for another use) and return the measured quantity to the saucepan. Add lemon juice and calcium water and mix well.
7. In a separate bowl, combine sugar and pectin powder. Mix thoroughly and set aside.
8. Bring the blueberry mixture back to a full boil over high heat. Slowly add pectin-sugar mixture, stirring constantly. Continue to stir vigorously for 1 to 2 minutes to dissolve pectin while the conserve comes back up to a boil. Once the conserve returns to a full boil, remove it from the heat.
9. **Can Your Conserve:** Remove jars from canner and ladle hot conserve into hot jars, leaving ¼ inch (6 mm) of headspace. Remove trapped air bubbles, wipe rims with a damp cloth, put on lids and screw bands, and tighten to fingertip tight. Lower filled jars into canner, ensuring jars are not touching each other and are covered with at least 1 to 2 inches (2.5 to 5 cm) of water. Place lid on canner, return to a rolling boil, and process for 10 minutes (adjusting for altitude if necessary). Turn off heat and allow canner to sit untouched for 5 minutes, then remove jars and allow to cool undisturbed for 12 to 24 hours. Confirm that jars have sealed, then store properly.

YIELD: 4 TO 5 HALF-PINT (8-OUNCE, OR 236 ML) JARS

KEEP IT EQUAL

If you have too much fruit and need to get rid of some to meet the required 4-cup (946 ml) quantity, be sure that you remove solids and liquids equally. This is very important in maintaining both the proper consistency and proper acidity of the final product. Don't pour off the liquid—instead, remove extra solids and liquids from the measuring cup one spoonful at a time, making an effort to remove liquid spoonfuls and solid spoonfuls in roughly equal quantities.

JALAPEÑO HEAT

In hot peppers, a lot of heat is in the seeds, which is one reason they're usually removed. If you like a little extra kick, feel free to leave a couple of the seeds in (but do not increase the overall quantity of pepper in the recipe). Also, don't forget to wear gloves when handling the jalapeños to protect your skin from the heat!

SAVORY ISLAND-SPICE CONSERVE

If you like Jamaican jerk–style seasoning, you'll love this conserve. Inspired by these island flavors, a potent blend of sweet and sour, along with earthy, savory spiciness and a little bit of heat. It makes an excellent glaze or accompaniment for grilled meats, vegetables, or savory pastries such as empanadas. Remember, for canning safety, do not increase the quantities of any of the vegetables or spices in this recipe, and be sure to use bottled lime juice.

||||||||||||||||||||||||||||||||||||||||||||||||||||||||||||||||||||||||||||||||||||||||||||||||||||||||||||||||||||||||||||||||||||||||||||

3½ cups (578 g) chopped pineapple* (for more information, see "Persnickety Pineapples!" on page 132)

1 cup (160 g) diced onions

2½ tablespoons (20 g) peeled, finely grated ginger root (for more information, see "Grate That Ginger!" on page 125)

1 tablespoon (5.6 g) seeded, minced jalapeño pepper

1 tablespoon (10 g) minced garlic

1 teaspoon (1.9 g) ground allspice

½ teaspoon (1 g) ground cloves

½ teaspoon (3 g) salt

¼ teaspoon (0.6 g) ground cinnamon

¼ teaspoon (0.7 g) ground nutmeg

1¼ cups (296 ml) water

¾ cup (175 ml) lime juice

2 teaspoons (10 ml) calcium water**

2 tablespoons (30 ml) dark rum (optional)

1¾ cups (263 g) unpacked brown sugar

2 teaspoons (6 g) Pomona's pectin powder

*Not sure how much fruit to purchase? See "Measuring Up!" on page 26.

**For information on how to prepare calcium water, refer to page 22.

1. If you are new to canning, or need a refresher, refer to chapter 1 (pages 12–41) for step-by-step guidance and additional information on how to safely can your conserve. Once ready, proceed as follows.
2. Prepare your jars, lids, and bands; heat up your canner; and sterilize your jars.
3. In a saucepan, combine chopped pineapple, onion, ginger, jalapeño pepper, garlic, allspice, cloves, salt, cinnamon, nutmeg, and the 1¼ cups (296 ml) water. Bring to a boil over high heat, reduce heat, and simmer, covered, for 20 minutes, stirring occasionally. Remove from heat.
4. Measure 4 cups (946 ml) of the cooked pineapple mixture (saving any extra for another use) and return the measured quantity to the saucepan. Add the lime juice, calcium water, and rum. Mix well.
5. In a separate bowl, combine sugar and pectin powder. Mix thoroughly and set aside.
6. Bring the fruit mixture to a full boil over high heat. Slowly add sugar-pectin mixture, stirring constantly. Continue to stir vigorously for 1 to 2 minutes to dissolve pectin while the conserve comes back up to a boil. Once the conserve returns to a full boil, remove it from the heat.
7. **Can Your Conserve:** Remove jars from canner and ladle hot conserve into hot jars, leaving ¼ inch (6 mm) of headspace. Remove trapped air bubbles, wipe rims with a damp cloth, put on lids and screw bands, and tighten to fingertip tight. Lower filled jars into canner, ensuring jars are not touching each other and are covered with at least 1 to 2 inches (2.5 to 5 cm) of water. Place lid on canner, return to a rolling boil, and process for 10 minutes (adjusting for altitude if necessary). Turn off heat and allow canner to sit untouched for 5 minutes, then remove jars and allow to cool undisturbed for 12 to 24 hours. Confirm that jars have sealed, then store properly.

YIELD: 4 TO 5 HALF-PINT (8-OUNCE, OR 236 ML) JARS

SAVORY SPICED-MANGO CONSERVE

If you're a fan of chutney, give this conserve a try! Inspired by the classic Indian condiment, this conserve melds the sweetness of mangoes with the earthy, complex flavors of garlic, ginger, and a variety of other spices. Remember, for canning safety, it's important that you do not increase the quantities of any of the vegetables or spices in this recipe, and be sure to use bottled lemon juice.

2 pounds (910 g) ripe, firm mangoes*

⅔ cup (110 g) diced onion

2 teaspoons (5.4 g) peeled, finely grated ginger root (for more information, see "Grate That Ginger!" on page 125)

1 teaspoon (3 g) minced garlic

¾ cup (175 ml) water

¾ cup (175 ml) white vinegar

½ cup (73 g) golden raisins (or dark raisins, if you prefer)

1½ teaspoons (3 g) ground coriander

1 teaspoon (3.7 g) mustard seed

½ teaspoon (1.25 g) ground cinnamon

½ teaspoon (1.2 g) ground turmeric

¼ teaspoon (0.6 g) ground cumin

⅛ teaspoon (0.15 g) hot pepper flakes

¼ teaspoon (1.5 g) salt

3 tablespoons (45 ml) lemon juice

2 teaspoons (10 ml) calcium water**

1⅓ cups (267 g) sugar

2 teaspoons (6 g) Pomona's pectin powder

*Not sure how much fruit to purchase? See "Measuring Up!" on page 26.

**For information on how to prepare calcium water, refer to page 22.

1. If you are new to canning, or need a refresher, refer to chapter 1 (pages 12–41) for step-by-step guidance and additional information on how to safely can your conserve. Once ready, proceed as follows.
2. Prepare your jars, lids, and bands; heat up your canner; and sterilize your jars.
3. Peel, pit, and dice mangoes. (For more information, see "Mango Madness!" on page 63.)
4. In a saucepan, combine mangoes, onion, ginger, garlic, the ¾ cup (175 ml) water, vinegar, raisins, coriander, mustard seeds, cinnamon, turmeric, cumin, hot pepper flakes, and salt. Bring to a boil over high heat, reduce heat, and then simmer, covered, for 20 minutes, stirring occasionally. Remove from heat.
5. Measure 4 cups (946 ml) of the cooked mango mixture (saving any extra for another use), and return the measured quantity to the saucepan. Add the lemon juice and calcium water and mix well.
6. In a separate bowl, combine sugar and pectin powder. Mix thoroughly and set aside.
7. Bring the mango mixture back to a full boil over high heat. Slowly add sugar-pectin mixture, stirring constantly. Continue to stir vigorously for 1 to 2 minutes to dissolve pectin while the conserve comes back up to a boil. Once the conserve returns to a full boil, remove it from the heat.
8. **Can Your Conserve:** Remove jars from canner and ladle hot conserve into hot jars, leaving ¼ inch (6 mm) of headspace. Remove trapped air bubbles, wipe rims with a damp cloth, put on lids and screw bands, and tighten to fingertip tight. Lower filled jars into canner, ensuring jars are not touching each other and are covered with at least 1 to 2 inches (2.5 to 5 cm) of water. Place lid on canner, return to a rolling boil, and process for 10 minutes (adjusting for altitude if necessary). Turn off heat and allow canner to sit untouched for 5 minutes, then remove jars and allow to cool undisturbed for 12 to 24 hours. Confirm that jars have sealed, then store properly.

YIELD: 4 TO 5 HALF-PINT (8-OUNCE, OR 236 ML) JARS

KEEP IT EQUAL

If you have too much fruit and need to get rid of some to meet the required 4-cup (946 ml) quantity, be sure that you remove solids and liquids equally. This is very important in maintaining both the proper consistency and proper acidity of the final product. Don't pour off the liquid—instead, remove extra solids and liquids from the measuring cup one spoonful at a time, making an effort to remove liquid spoonfuls and solid spoonfuls in roughly equal quantities.

TROPICAL CONSERVE

For a little taste of the tropics, give this delightful conserve a try. Mango, pineapple, and orange make it naturally sweet, while the coconut, cashews, and raisins give it a satisfying chewy, crunchy texture. I like this conserve to be golden in color, so I opt for golden raisins, but you can use dark raisins if you prefer. Try this conserve as a filling for fruit bars—with a tropical twist!

1 pound (455 g) ripe, firm mangoes*

1½ cups (248 g) chopped pineapple* (for more information, see "Persnickety Pineapples!" on page 132)

1 medium orange, peeled and chopped

½ cup (35 g) dried, shredded, unsweetened coconut

⅔ cup (97 g) golden raisins (or dark raisins, if you prefer)

½ cup (115 g) coarsely chopped raw cashews

1¾ cups (414 ml) water

½ cup (120 ml) lemon juice

4 teaspoons (20 ml) calcium water**

¾ cup (150 g) sugar

3 teaspoons (9 g) Pomona's pectin powder

*Not sure how much fruit to purchase? See "Measuring Up!" on page 26.

**For information on how to prepare calcium water, refer to page 22.

1. If you are new to canning, or need a refresher, refer to chapter 1 (pages 12–41) for step-by-step guidance and additional information on how to safely can your conserve. Once ready, proceed as follows.
2. Prepare your jars, lids, and bands; heat up your canner; and sterilize your jars.
3. Peel, pit, and dice mangoes. (For more information, see "Mango Madness!" on page 63.)
4. Combine mango, pineapple, orange, coconut, raisins, cashews, and the 1¾ cups (414 ml) water in a saucepan. Bring to a boil over high heat, reduce heat, and then simmer, covered, for 20 minutes, or until fruit is soft, stirring occasionally. Remove from heat.
5. Measure 4 cups (946 ml) of the cooked fruit (saving any extra for another use), and return measured quantity to the saucepan. Add lemon juice and calcium water, and mix well.
6. In a separate bowl, combine sugar and pectin powder. Mix thoroughly and set aside.
7. Bring fruit mixture back to a full boil over high heat. Slowly add pectin-sugar mixture, stirring constantly. Continue to stir vigorously for 1 to 2 minutes to dissolve pectin while the conserve comes back up to a boil. Once the conserve returns to a full boil, remove it from the heat.
8. **Can Your Conserve:** Remove jars from canner and ladle hot conserve into hot jars, leaving ¼ inch (6 mm) of headspace. Remove trapped air bubbles, wipe rims with a damp cloth, put on lids and screw bands, and tighten to fingertip tight. Lower filled jars into canner, ensuring jars are not touching each other and are covered with at least 1 to 2 inches (2.5 to 5 cm) of water. Place lid on canner, return to a rolling boil, and process for 10 minutes (adjusting for altitude if necessary). Turn off heat and allow canner to sit untouched for 5 minutes, then remove jars and allow to cool undisturbed for 12 to 24 hours. Confirm that jars have sealed, then store properly.

YIELD: 4 TO 5 HALF-PINT (8-OUNCE, OR 236 ML) JARS

IT'S IN THE CAN!

You can substitute canned pineapple for the fresh if that's all you have, or you want to save a little time on prep work. Simply drain canned, unsweetened pineapple chunks (discard the juice or save it for another use) and then chop them.

CHERRY-AMARETTO CONSERVE

The lusciousness of fresh cherries combined with the sweet warmth and depth of amaretto really make this conserve shine. Almonds and raisins add a toothsome, chewy yet crunchy texture. For a simple but elegant dessert, layer this conserve with vanilla ice cream and whipped cream in a parfait glass, and top with some extra sliced almonds.

1¾ pounds (794 g) sweet cherries*

½ cup (73 g) golden raisins (or dark raisins, if you prefer)

½ cup (63 g) sliced almonds

1 cup (235 ml) amaretto liqueur

¼ cup (60 ml) lemon juice

4 teaspoons (20 ml) calcium water**

¾ cup (150 g) sugar

3 teaspoons (9 g) Pomona's pectin powder

Not sure how much fruit to purchase? See "Measuring Up!" on page 26.

**For information on how to prepare calcium water, refer to page 22.*

1. If you are new to canning, or need a refresher, refer to chapter 1 (pages 12–41) for step-by-step guidance and additional information on how to safely can your conserve. Once ready, proceed as follows.
2. Prepare your jars, lids, and bands; heat up your canner; and sterilize your jars.
3. Rinse cherries, remove stems, slice in half, and remove pits. (For more information, see "Painless Pitting" on page 70.)
4. Combine cherry halves in a saucepan with raisins, almonds, and amaretto. Bring to a boil over high heat, reduce heat, and simmer, covered, for 5 minutes, stirring occasionally. Remove from heat.
5. Measure 4 cups (946 ml) of the cooked cherry mixture (saving any extra for another use), and return the measured quantity to the saucepan. Add lemon juice and calcium water, and mix well.
6. In a separate bowl, combine sugar and pectin powder. Mix thoroughly and set aside.
7. Bring cherry mixture back to a full boil over high heat. Slowly add pectin-sugar mixture, stirring constantly. Continue to stir vigorously for 1 to 2 minutes to dissolve pectin while the conserve comes back up to a boil. Once the conserve returns to a full boil, remove it from the heat.
8. **Can Your Conserve:** Remove jars from canner and ladle hot conserve into hot jars, leaving ¼ inch (6 mm) of headspace. Remove trapped air bubbles, wipe rims with a damp cloth, put on lids and screw bands, and tighten to fingertip tight. Lower filled jars into canner, ensuring jars are not touching each other and are covered with at least 1 to 2 inches (2.5 to 5 cm) of water. Place lid on canner, return to a rolling boil, and process for 10 minutes (adjusting for altitude if necessary). Turn off heat and allow canner to sit untouched for 5 minutes, then remove jars and allow to cool undisturbed for 12 to 24 hours. Confirm that jars have sealed, then store properly.

YIELD: 4 TO 5 HALF-PINT (8-OUNCE, OR 236 ML) JARS

CUSTOMIZE IT!

If you prefer a less-processed sugar, such as turbinado (raw sugar), you can use that instead of regular white sugar. Just be sure to pulse it in a food processor a few times to make the granules fine enough that you'll be able to mix the pectin into the sugar effectively.

HONEYED APRICOT-DATE-ALMOND CONSERVE

Inspired by some of the classic flavors of the Mediterranean and the Middle East, this rich, sweet conserve is a real treat. Swirl it into a steaming bowl of oatmeal, spoon it over a chilled bowl of coconut rice pudding, or enjoy it as a filling for crunchy, chewy cookie bars—no matter how you have it, it's simply delightful!

2 pounds (910 g) ripe apricots*

½ cup (90 g) finely chopped, dried dates

½ cup (63 g) sliced almonds

½ cup (120 ml) water

⅓ cup (75 ml) lemon juice

4 teaspoons (20 ml) calcium water**

½ cup (170 g) honey

3 teaspoons (9 g) Pomona's pectin powder

*Not sure how much fruit to purchase? See "Measuring Up!" on page 26.

**For information on how to prepare calcium water, refer to page 22.

CUSTOMIZE IT!

If you're looking for something new, try spicing it up! At the same time that you add the calcium water, add up to 1 teaspoon (2.5 g) of ground ginger, cardamom, cloves, cinnamon, nutmeg, or allspice, Or, you can mix and match these spices—just be sure that the total spice quantity does not exceed 1 teaspoon (2.5 g).

1. If you are new to canning, or need a refresher, refer to chapter 1 (pages 12–41) for step-by-step guidance and additional information on how to safely can your conserve. Once ready, proceed as follows.
2. Prepare your jars, lids, and bands; heat up your canner; and sterilize your jars.
3. Rinse apricots, remove stems, and then slice in half or pull apart. Remove pits, and then dice apricots. (For more information, see "To Peel or Not to Peel?" on page 76.)
4. Combine diced apricots in a saucepan with chopped dates, sliced almonds, and the ½ cup (120 ml) water. Bring to a boil over high heat, reduce heat, and simmer, covered, 5 to 10 minutes, or until fruit is soft, stirring occasionally. Remove from heat.
5. Measure out 4 cups (946 ml) of the cooked mixture (saving any extra for another use), and return the measured quantity to the saucepan. Add the lemon juice and calcium water, and mix well.
6. In a separate bowl, combine honey and pectin powder. Mix thoroughly and set aside.
7. Bring fruit mixture back to a full boil over high heat. Slowly add pectin-honey mixture, stirring constantly. Continue to stir vigorously for 1 to 2 minutes to dissolve pectin while the conserve comes back up to a boil. Once the conserve returns to a full boil, remove it from the heat.
8. **Can Your Conserve:** Remove jars from canner and ladle hot conserve into hot jars, leaving ¼ inch (6 mm) of headspace. Remove trapped air bubbles, wipe rims with a damp cloth, put on lids and screw bands, and tighten to fingertip tight. Lower filled jars into canner, ensuring jars are not touching each other and are covered with at least 1 to 2 inches (2.5 to 5 cm) of water. Place lid on canner, return to a rolling boil, and process for 10 minutes (adjusting for altitude if necessary). Turn off heat and allow canner to sit untouched for 5 minutes, then remove jars and allow to cool undisturbed for 12 to 24 hours. Confirm that jars have sealed, then store properly.

YIELD: 4 TO 5 HALF-PINT (8-OUNCE, OR 236 ML) JARS

PLUM-GINGER-ORANGE CONSERVE

The combination of orange, almond, and ginger melding with the sweet, rich tang of fresh plums makes this gorgeous purple conserve sing. Enjoy it atop shortcake cups, with a generous dollop of whipped cream—what a treat!

2 pounds (910 g) ripe, sweet plums*

1 tablespoon (14 g) finely chopped crystallized ginger

½ cup (63 g) sliced almonds

2 tablespoons (30 ml) orange liqueur (optional)

2 medium oranges, divided

¼ cup (60 ml) lemon juice

4 teaspoons (20 ml) calcium water**

1 cup (200 g) sugar

3 teaspoons (9 g) Pomona's pectin powder

*Not sure how much fruit to purchase? See "Measuring Up!" on page 26.

**For information on how to prepare calcium water, refer to page 22.

CRYSTALLIZE IT!

This recipe calls for crystallized ginger—essentially, slices of fresh ginger root that have been cooked and preserved with sugar. Crystallized ginger is easy and quick to chop, so it's very convenient in recipes. It's available at Asian markets and at many natural food stores.

1. If you are new to canning, or need a refresher, refer to chapter 1 (pages 12–41) for step-by-step guidance and additional information on how to safely can your conserve. Once ready, proceed as follows.
2. Prepare your jars, lids, and bands; heat up your canner; and sterilize your jars.
3. Rinse plums, remove stems, and slice in half. Remove pits, and dice plums. (For more information, see "To Peel or Not to Peel?" on page 76.) Combine diced plums in a saucepan with crystallized ginger, sliced almonds, and orange liqueur.
4. Slice 1 of the oranges in half and squeeze out its juice, discarding seeds and the peel. Add the juice to the plum mixture.
5. Wash the remaining orange. Using a vegetable peeler, slice off pieces of the outer part of the peel, and finely chop. Add 2 tablespoons (12 g) of the finely chopped peel to the plum mixture.
6. Remove the rest of the peel from the orange, and discard the remaining peel. Remove and discard seeds, any extra white pith, and any especially fibrous parts of the membrane from the fruit. Finely chop the flesh of the fruit, and then add to the plum mixture.
7. Bring fruit mixture to a boil over high heat, reduce heat, and simmer, covered, for 10 to 12 minutes, or until peel is soft, stirring occasionally. Remove from heat.
8. Measure 4 cups (946 ml) of the fruit mixture (saving any extra for another use) and return the measured quantity to the saucepan. Add the lemon juice and calcium water and mix well.
9. In a separate bowl, combine sugar and pectin powder. Mix and set aside.
10. Bring fruit mixture back to a full boil over high heat. Slowly add pectin-sugar mixture, stirring constantly. Continue to stir vigorously for 1 to 2 minutes to dissolve pectin while the conserve comes back up to a boil. Once the conserve returns to a full boil, remove from heat.
11. **Can Your Conserve:** Remove jars from canner and ladle hot conserve into hot jars, leaving ¼ inch (6 mm) of headspace. Remove trapped air bubbles, wipe rims with a damp cloth, put on lids and screw bands, and tighten to fingertip tight. Lower filled jars into canner, ensuring jars are not touching each other and are covered with at least 1 to 2 inches (2.5 to 5 cm) of water. Place lid on canner, return to a rolling boil, and process for 10 minutes (adjusting for altitude if necessary). Turn off heat and allow canner to sit untouched for 5 minutes, then remove jars and allow to cool undisturbed for 12 to 24 hours. Confirm that jars have sealed, then store properly.

YIELD: 4 TO 5 HALF-PINT (8-OUNCE, OR 236 ML) JARS

APPLE-RAISIN-WALNUT CONSERVE

I never tire of the combination of apples, raisins, and walnuts, along with a touch of autumnal spice, and this conserve is a wonderful way to enjoy the fresh, local apples that are abundant during fall. For a delicious, eye-catching fall or winter dessert, use this conserve as a filling for a lattice-top pie.

1½ pounds (680 g) hard, crisp apples*

½ cup (73 g) raisins

½ cup (59 g) chopped walnuts

½ teaspoon (1.25 g) ground cinnamon

¼ teaspoon (0.7 g) ground nutmeg

⅛ teaspoon (0.4 g) ground cloves

⅛ teaspoon (0.35 g) ground ginger

2¼ cups (530 ml) water

¼ cup (60 ml) lemon juice

4 teaspoons (20 ml) calcium water**

¾ cup (150 g) sugar

3 teaspoons (9 g) Pomona's pectin powder

*Not sure how much fruit to purchase? See "Measuring Up!" on page 26.

**For information on how to prepare calcium water, refer to page 22.

1. If you are new to canning, or need a refresher, refer to chapter 1 (pages 12–41) for step-by-step guidance and additional information on how to safely can your conserve. Once ready, proceed as follows.
2. Prepare your jars, lids, and bands; heat up your canner; and sterilize your jars.
3. Peel apples, remove stems and cores, and dice. Combine diced apples in a saucepan with raisins, walnuts, cinnamon, nutmeg, cloves, ginger, and the 2¼ cups (530 ml) water. Bring to a boil over high heat, reduce heat, and simmer, covered, for 5 to 10 minutes, or until fruit is soft, stirring occasionally. Remove from heat.
4. Measure 4 cups (946 ml) of the cooked mixture (saving any extra for another use), and return the measured quantity to the saucepan. Add lemon juice and calcium water, and mix well.
5. In a separate bowl, combine sugar and pectin powder. Mix thoroughly and set aside.
6. Bring apple mixture back to a full boil over high heat. Slowly add pectin-sugar mixture, stirring constantly. Continue to stir vigorously for 1 to 2 minutes to dissolve pectin while the conserve comes back up to a boil. Once the conserve returns to a full boil, remove it from the heat.
7. **Can Your Conserve:** Remove jars from canner and ladle hot conserve into hot jars, leaving ¼ inch (6 mm) of headspace. Remove trapped air bubbles, wipe rims with a damp cloth, put on lids and screw bands, and tighten to fingertip tight. Lower filled jars into canner, ensuring jars are not touching each other and are covered with at least 1 to 2 inches (2.5 to 5 cm) of water. Place lid on canner, return to a rolling boil, and process for 10 minutes (adjusting for altitude if necessary). Turn off heat and allow canner to sit untouched for 5 minutes, then remove jars and allow to cool undisturbed for 12 to 24 hours. Confirm that jars have sealed, then store properly.

YIELD: 4 TO 5 HALF-PINT (8-OUNCE, OR 236 ML) JARS

GO FOR THE CRUNCH!

Use hard, crisp apples in this recipe so that the fruit will retain its shape when cooked—Granny Smiths work well.

VANILLA-RHUBARB-NECTARINE CONSERVE

Fresh vanilla beautifully showcases the pleasing sweetness of nectarines, while tempering the assertive tang of rhubarb in this conserve. Swirl this unexpected combination into plain yogurt to brighten up your breakfast, or enjoy it on top of vanilla ice cream for an easy weeknight dessert.

1½ pounds (680 g) ripe nectarines*

¾ pound (340 g) trimmed rhubarb stalks*

⅔ cup (100 g) golden raisins (or dark raisins, if you prefer)

½ cup (59 g) chopped walnuts

¾ cup (175 ml) water

1 vanilla bean

¼ cup (60 ml) lemon juice

4 teaspoons (20 ml) calcium water**

1½ cups (300 g) sugar

3 teaspoons (9 g) Pomona's pectin powder

*Not sure how much fruit to purchase? See "Measuring Up!" on page 26.

**For information on how to prepare your calcium water, refer to page 24.

1. If you are new to canning, or need a refresher, refer to chapter 1 (pages 12–41) for step-by-step guidance and additional information on how to safely can your conserve. Once ready, proceed as follows.
2. Prepare your jars, lids, and bands; heat up your canner; and sterilize your jars.
3. Peel and remove pits from the nectarines, and then dice. (For more information, see "How to Skin a Peach" on page 58.)
4. Rinse rhubarb, slice stalks lengthwise into thin strips, and then dice.
5. Combine diced nectarines, diced rhubarb, raisins, walnuts, and the ¾ cup (175 ml) water in a saucepan. Using a paring knife, slice the vanilla bean pod in half lengthwise and scrape out the seeds. Add the vanilla seeds and the bean pod itself to the mixture. Bring mixture to a boil over high heat, reduce heat, and simmer, covered, for 5 to 10 minutes, or until fruit is soft, stirring occasionally. Remove from heat.
6. Measure 4 cups (946 ml) of the cooked mixture (saving any extra for another use), and return the measured quantity to the saucepan. Add the lemon juice and calcium water, and mix well.
7. In a separate bowl, combine sugar and pectin powder. Mix thoroughly and set aside.
8. Bring fruit mixture back to a full boil over high heat. Slowly add pectin-sugar mixture, stirring constantly. Continue to stir vigorously for 1 to 2 minutes to dissolve pectin while the conserve comes back up to a boil. Once the conserve returns to a full boil, remove it from the heat. Using tongs, carefully remove and discard the vanilla bean pod.
9. **Can Your Conserve:** Remove jars from canner and ladle hot conserve into hot jars, leaving ¼ inch (6 mm) of headspace. Remove trapped air bubbles, wipe rims with a damp cloth, put on lids and screw bands, and tighten to fingertip tight. Lower filled jars into canner, ensuring jars are not touching each other and are covered with at least 1 to 2 inches (2.5 to 5 cm) of water. Place lid on canner, return to a rolling boil, and process for 10 minutes (adjusting for altitude if necessary). Turn off heat and allow canner to sit untouched for 5 minutes, then remove jars and allow to cool undisturbed for 12 to 24 hours. Confirm that jars have sealed, then store properly.

YIELD: 4 TO 5 HALF-PINT (8-OUNCE, OR 236 ML) JARS

CUSTOMIZE IT!

If you're looking for something new, why not try honey instead of sugar? In place of the sugar in this recipe, use ½ to 1 cup (170 to 340 g) honey.

Chapter 6

MARMALADES

||||||||||||||||||||||||||||||||||||||||||||||||||||||||||||||||||||||||||||||||||||||||||||||||||||||

If there's a renegade in the bunch of jelled products, marmalade is it. In the midst of so many sweet, pleasant, eminently likeable jams and jellies, marmalade is unabashed when it comes to her sometimes affronting nature. With the sweet and sour of citrus fruit, sharply contrasting with the bitterness of the peel—some of which is almost always included— marmalade is often an acquired taste. But those who acquire it tend to acquire it passionately. That's certainly true for me! I find marmalades to be a soulful, intriguing combination of straight-up sweetness, beautifully tempered by just the right amount of sour and bitter.

SIMPLE CLASSIC: ORANGE MARMALADE

There are many time-consuming, complicated marmalade recipes out there—but this is not one of them! This recipe for classic orange marmalade is remarkably simple, and the results are delicious. One of my favorite things about marmalade, and what sets it apart from many other jams and jellies, is its delicate balance between bitter and sweet. It's really quite lovely as a topping on vanilla ice cream or blended into your morning fruit and yogurt smoothie.

6 medium-size oranges

3 cups (710 ml) water

3 tablespoons (45 ml) lemon juice

3 teaspoons (15 ml) calcium water*

2½ cups (500 g) sugar

4½ teaspoons (13.5 g) Pomona's pectin powder

*For information on how to prepare calcium water, refer to page 22.

1. If you are new to canning, or need a refresher, refer to chapter 1 (pages 12–41) for step-by-step guidance and additional information on how to safely can your marmalade. Once ready, proceed as follows.
2. Prepare your jars, lids, and bands; heat up your canner; and sterilize your jars.
3. Thoroughly wash the oranges. Peel the fruit, and set aside the peels from 2 of the oranges, discarding the remaining peels. Remove and discard any seeds, excess white pith, or especially fibrous parts of the membrane from the flesh of all the oranges. Finely chop the flesh of all the oranges.
4. Using a paring knife, scrape off and discard the inner white part of the peels. Slice the peels into thin strips, about 1-inch (2.5 cm) long.
5. In a large saucepan, combine chopped fruit, sliced peels, and the 3 cups (710 ml) of water. Bring mixture to a boil over high heat. Reduce heat and simmer, covered, for 20 minutes, stirring occasionally. Remove from heat.
6. Measure 6 cups (1.4 L) of the cooked fruit (saving any extra for another use), and return the measured quantity to the saucepan. Add lemon juice and calcium water and mix well.
7. In a separate bowl, combine sugar and pectin powder. Mix thoroughly and set aside.
8. Bring fruit mixture back to a full boil over high heat. Slowly add pectin-sugar mixture, stirring constantly. Continue to stir vigorously for 1 to 2 minutes to dissolve pectin while the marmalade comes back up to a boil. Once the marmalade returns to a full boil, remove it from the heat.
9. **Can Your Marmalade:** Remove jars from canner and ladle hot marmalade into hot jars, leaving ¼ inch (6 mm) of headspace. Remove trapped air bubbles, wipe rims with a damp cloth, put on lids and screw bands, and tighten to fingertip tight. Lower filled jars into canner, ensuring jars are not touching each other and are covered with at least 1 to 2 inches (2.5 to 5 cm) of water. Place lid on canner, return to a rolling boil, and process for 10 minutes (adjusting for altitude if necessary). Turn off heat and allow canner to sit untouched for 5 minutes, then remove jars and allow to cool undisturbed for 12 to 24 hours. Confirm that jars have sealed, then store properly.

YIELD: 6 TO 7 HALF-PINT (8-OUNCE, OR 236 ML) JARS

CUSTOMIZE IT!

If you're looking for something new, why not try honey instead of sugar? In place of the sugar in this recipe, use 1 up to 1½ cups (340 to 510 g) honey.

HILLARY'S PINEAPPLE-ORANGE MARMALADE

After trying orange marmalade for the first time, my young niece Hillary told me that I should make one with pineapple, and just like that the idea for this marmalade was born. The natural bitterness of the orange peel is perfectly tempered by the intense sweetness of the fresh pineapple in this lovely, golden-orange marmalade. Enjoy on hearty whole-grain bread or—as Hillary does—on a warm English muffin with a pat of butter.

4 medium-size oranges

4½ cups (743 g) chopped pineapple (for more information, see "Persnickety Pineapples!" on page 132)

2¼ cups (530 ml) water

1½ tablespoons (22 ml) lemon juice

3 teaspoons (15 ml) calcium water*

1½ cups (300 g) sugar

3¾ teaspoons (11.25 g) Pomona's pectin powder

For information on how to prepare calcium water, refer to page 22.

1. If you are new to canning, or need a refresher, refer to chapter 1 (pages 12–41) for step-by-step guidance and additional information on how to safely can your marmalade. Once ready, proceed as follows.
2. Prepare your jars, lids, and bands; heat up your canner; and sterilize your jars.
3. Thoroughly wash the oranges. Peel the fruit and set aside peels from 2 of the oranges, discarding the remaining peels. Remove and discard any seeds, excess white pith, or especially fibrous parts of the membrane from the flesh of all the oranges. Finely chop the flesh of all the oranges.
4. Using a paring knife, scrape off and discard the inner white part of the reserved peels. Slice the peels into thin strips, about 1-inch (2.5 cm) long.
5. In a saucepan, combine the chopped oranges, chopped pineapple, sliced peels, and the 2¼ cups (530 ml) of water. Bring mixture to a boil. Reduce heat and simmer, covered, for 20 minutes, stirring occasionally. Remove from heat.
6. Measure out 6 cups (1.4 L) of the cooked fruit mixture (saving any remaining fruit for another use), and return the measured quantity to the saucepan. Add lemon juice and calcium water, and mix well.
7. In a separate bowl, combine sugar and pectin powder. Mix thoroughly and set aside.
8. Bring fruit mixture back to a full boil over high heat. Slowly add pectin-sugar mixture, stirring constantly. Continue to stir vigorously for 1 to 2 minutes to dissolve pectin while the marmalade comes back up to a boil. Once the marmalade returns to a full boil, remove it from the heat.
9. **Can Your Marmalade:** Remove jars from canner and ladle hot marmalade into hot jars, leaving ¼ inch (6 mm) of headspace. Remove trapped air bubbles, wipe rims with a damp cloth, put on lids and screw bands, and tighten to fingertip tight. Lower filled jars into canner, ensuring jars are not touching each other and are covered with at least 1 to 2 inches (2.5 to 5 cm) of water. Place lid on canner, return to a rolling boil, and process for 10 minutes (adjusting for altitude if necessary). Turn off heat and allow canner to sit untouched for 5 minutes, then remove jars and allow to cool undisturbed for 12 to 24 hours. Confirm that jars have sealed, then store properly.

YIELD: 6 TO 7 HALF-PINT (8-OUNCE, OR 236 ML) JARS

IT'S IN THE CAN!

You can substitute canned pineapple for the fresh if that's all you have, or you want to save a little time on prep work. Simply drain unsweetened canned pineapple chunks (discard the juice or save it for another use) and then chop them.

ORANGE-RHUBARB MARMALADE

"My parents have a big patch of rhubarb that comes up every year—more than we know what to do with—so that was the inspiration for the recipe," says jam-maker Heidi Butler. This marmalade, adapted from Heidi's recipe, is, indeed, a delicious way to keep on top of an overly abundant rhubarb patch. The sweetness of the orange and the mild bitterness of its skin are a perfect counterpoint to the tartness of the rhubarb.

||||||||||||||||||||||||||||||||||||||||||||||||||||||||||||||||||||||||||||||||||||||||||||||||||||||||||||||||||||||||

4 medium-size oranges

1½ pounds (680 g) trimmed rhubarb stalks*

3 cups (710 ml) water

4½ tablespoons (66.5 ml) lemon juice

3 teaspoons (15 ml) calcium water**

2½ cups (500 g) sugar

4½ teaspoons (13.5 g) Pomona's pectin powder

*Not sure how much fruit to purchase? See "Measuring Up!" on page 26.

**For information on how to prepare calcium water, refer to page 22.

1. If you are new to canning, or need a refresher, refer to chapter 1 (pages 12–41) for step-by-step guidance and additional information on how to safely can your marmalade. Once ready, proceed as follows.
2. Prepare your jars, lids, and bands; heat up your canner; and sterilize your jars.
3. Thoroughly wash the oranges. Peel the fruit and set aside peels from 2 of the oranges, discarding the remaining peels. Remove and discard any seeds, excess white pith, or especially fibrous parts of the membrane from the flesh of all the oranges. Finely chop the flesh of all the oranges.
4. Using a paring knife, scrape off and discard the inner white part of the reserved peels. Slice the peels into thin strips, about 1-inch (2.5 cm) long.
5. Rinse rhubarb thoroughly. Slice stalks lengthwise into thin strips, and then dice.
6. In a large saucepan, combine chopped oranges, diced rhubarb, sliced peels, and the 3 cups (710 ml) of water. Bring mixture to a boil over high heat, reduce heat, and simmer, covered, for 20 minutes, stirring occasionally. Remove from heat.
7. Measure 6 cups (1.4 L) of the cooked fruit mixture (saving any remaining fruit for another use), and return the measured quantity to the saucepan. Add lemon juice and calcium water, and mix well.
8. In a separate bowl, combine sugar and pectin powder. Mix thoroughly and set aside.
9. Bring fruit back to a full boil over high heat. Slowly add pectin-sugar mixture, stirring constantly. Continue to stir vigorously for 1 to 2 minutes to dissolve pectin while the marmalade comes back up to a boil. Once the marmalade returns to a full boil, remove it from the heat.
10. **Can Your Marmalade:** Remove jars from canner and ladle hot marmalade into hot jars, leaving ¼ inch (6 mm) of headspace. Remove trapped air bubbles, wipe rims with a damp cloth, put on lids and screw bands, and tighten to fingertip tight. Lower filled jars into canner, ensuring jars are not touching each other and are covered with at least 1 to 2 inches (2.5 to 5 cm) of water. Place lid on canner, return to a rolling boil, and process for 10 minutes (adjusting for altitude if necessary). Turn off heat and allow canner to sit untouched for 5 minutes, then remove jars and allow to cool undisturbed for 12 to 24 hours. Confirm that jars have sealed, then store properly.

YIELD: 6 TO 7 HALF-PINT (8-OUNCE, OR 236 ML) JARS

||||||||||||||||||||||||||||||||||||||||||||||||||||||||||||||||||||||||||||||||||

FREEZE IT!

I enjoy making marmalades in the winter because their flavor is best when citrus is at its peak, but winter is not exactly rhubarb season. Fortunately, rhubarb freezes beautifully, and is a great way to preserve any extra you might have for later use. Trim it, wash it, dice it, and pop it in the freezer. Then you'll have rhubarb ready to go whenever you want to make this marmalade or any of the other recipes in this book that call for rhubarb!

||||||||||||||||||||||||||||||||||||||||||||||||||||||||||||||||||||||

GINGERED ZUCCHINI-ORANGE MARMALADE

This delicious marmalade is an excellent way to make use of a bountiful zucchini harvest. The more assertive flavors of orange and ginger are a perfect complement to the subtle flavor of the zucchini in this delightful, green-flecked spread. For canning safety, do not increase the quantity of zucchini or ginger in this recipe, and remember to use bottled lemon juice.

||||||||||||||||||||||||||||||||||||||||||||||||||||||||||||||||||||||||||||||||||||||||||||||||||||||||||||||||||||||||||||||||||||||

3 medium-size oranges

5 cups (670 g) grated zucchini

2 tablespoons (16 g) peeled, finely grated ginger root (for more information, see "Grate That Ginger!" on page 125)

2½ cups (570 ml) orange juice

⅔ cup (158 ml) lemon juice

3 teaspoons (15 ml) calcium water*

2 cups (400 g) sugar

5 teaspoons (15 g) Pomona's pectin powder

*For information on how to prepare calcium water, refer to page 22.

KEEP IT EQUAL

If you have too much fruit and need to get rid of some to meet the required 5¾-cup (1.36 L) quantity, be sure that you remove solids and liquids equally. This is very important in maintaining both the proper consistency and proper acidity of the final product. Don't pour off the liquid—instead, remove extra solids and liquids from the measuring cup one spoonful at a time, making an effort to remove liquid spoonfuls and solid spoonfuls in roughly equal quantities.

1. If you are new to canning, or need a refresher, refer to chapter 1 (pages 12–41) for step-by-step guidance and additional information on how to safely can your marmalade. Once ready, proceed as follows.

2. Prepare your jars, lids, and bands; heat up your canner; and sterilize your jars.

3. Thoroughly wash the oranges. Peel the fruit and set aside the peels from 2 of the oranges, discarding the remaining peel. Remove and discard any seeds, excess white pith, or especially fibrous parts of the membrane from the flesh of all the oranges. Finely chop the flesh of all the oranges.

4. Using a paring knife, scrape off and discard the inner white part of the reserved peels. Slice the peels into thin strips, about 1-inch (2.5 cm) long.

5. In a large saucepan, combine chopped oranges, sliced peels, grated zucchini, grated ginger, and orange juice. Bring mixture to a boil over high heat, reduce heat, and simmer, covered, for 20 minutes, stirring occasionally.

6. Remove pan from heat. Measure 5¾ cups (1.36 L) of the cooked mixture (saving any extra for another use), and combine measured quantity in a saucepan with lemon juice and calcium water. Mix well.

7. In a separate bowl, combine sugar and pectin powder. Mix thoroughly and set aside.

8. Bring fruit back to a full boil over high heat. Slowly add pectin-sugar mixture, stirring constantly. Continue to stir vigorously for 1 to 2 minutes to dissolve pectin while the marmalade comes back up to a boil. Once the marmalade returns to a full boil, remove it from the heat.

9. **Can Your Marmalade:** Remove jars from canner and ladle hot marmalade into hot jars, leaving ¼ inch (6 mm) of headspace. Remove trapped air bubbles, wipe rims with a damp cloth, put on lids and screw bands, and tighten to fingertip tight. Lower filled jars into canner, ensuring jars are not touching each other and are covered with at least 1 to 2 inches (2.5 to 5 cm) of water. Place lid on canner, return to a rolling boil, and process for 10 minutes (adjusting for altitude if necessary). Turn off heat and allow canner to sit untouched for 5 minutes, then remove jars and allow to cool undisturbed for 12 to 24 hours. Confirm that jars have sealed, then store properly.

YIELD: 6 TO 7 HALF-PINT (8-OUNCE, OR 236 ML) JARS

CRANBERRY-GRAPEFRUIT MARMALADE

Grapefruit and cranberry are a delicious and unexpected combination, and together they make a gorgeous, red marmalade. The grapefruit peel and the whole cranberries contribute to the appealing, chunky texture, though if you prefer your cranberries chopped up, feel free to give them a whirl in your food processor before cooking. Slathered on any kind of muffin or toast, this sweet, sour, and assertive marmalade is the perfect wake-up call on a sleepy weekend morning.

4 medium-size grapefruits (white or pink)

1 bag (12 ounces, or 340 g) cranberries

3 cups (710 ml) water

3 tablespoons (45 ml) lemon juice

3 teaspoons (15 ml) calcium water*

2½ cups (500 g) sugar

4½ teaspoons (13.5 g) Pomona's pectin powder

For information on how to prepare calcium water, refer to page 22.

GO ORGANIC!

Buying organic is always a good idea, but it's especially important when you're planning to use the peel of the fruit, as nonorganic produce may have been sprayed with pesticides or other chemicals that are nearly impossible to wash off. So choose organic grapefruit if you can for this recipe—it will make a difference!

1. If you are new to canning, or need a refresher, refer to chapter 1 (pages 12–41) for step-by-step guidance and additional information on how to safely can your marmalade. Once ready, proceed as follows.
2. Prepare your jars, lids, and bands; heat up your canner; and sterilize your jars.
3. Thoroughly wash the grapefruits. Peel the fruit and set aside the peels from 1½ of the grapefruits, discarding the remaining peels. Remove and discard any seeds, excess white pith, or especially fibrous parts of the membrane from the flesh of all the grapefruits. Finely chop the flesh of all the grapefruits.
4. Using a paring knife, scrape off and discard the inner white part of the reserved peels. Slice the peels into thin strips, about 1-inch (2.5 cm) long.
5. Rinse the cranberries. In a large saucepan, combine the cranberries with the chopped grapefruit, sliced peels, and the 3 cups (710 ml) of water. Bring mixture to a boil over high heat. Reduce heat and simmer, covered, for 20 minutes, stirring occasionally. Remove pan from heat.
6. Measure 6 cups (1.4 L) of the cooked fruit (saving any extra for another use), and return the measured quantity to the saucepan. Add lemon juice and calcium water and mix well.
7. In a separate bowl, combine sugar and pectin powder. Mix thoroughly and set aside.
8. Bring fruit mixture back to a full boil over high heat. Slowly add pectin-sugar mixture, stirring constantly. Continue to stir vigorously for 1 to 2 minutes to dissolve pectin while the marmalade comes back up to a boil. Once the marmalade returns to a full boil, remove it from the heat.
9. **Can Your Marmalade:** Remove jars from canner and ladle hot marmalade into hot jars, leaving ¼ inch (6 mm) of headspace. Remove trapped air bubbles, wipe rims with a damp cloth, put on lids and screw bands, and tighten to fingertip tight. Lower filled jars into canner, ensuring jars are not touching each other and are covered with at least 1 to 2 inches (2.5 to 5 cm) of water. Place lid on canner, return to a rolling boil, and process for 10 minutes (adjusting for altitude if necessary). Turn off heat and allow canner to sit untouched for 5 minutes, then remove jars and allow to cool undisturbed for 12 to 24 hours. Confirm that jars have sealed, then store properly.

YIELD: 6 TO 7 HALF-PINT (8-OUNCE, OR 236 ML) JARS

SUNRISE MARMALADE

I'm a huge fan of carrot cake, and if it's possible to have a marmalade version of that delectable dessert, this is it. It's lightly spiced and lusciously sweet, and spread generously on dark bread with a bit of butter, this delicious marmalade is a perfect way to greet the morning. For canning safety, don't increase the quantity of the carrots in this recipe, and remember to use bottled lemon juice.

2 medium-size oranges

1⅓ cups (147 g) peeled, grated carrots

1⅓ cups (220 g) chopped pineapple (for more information, see "Persnickety Pineapples!" on page 132)

¼ cup (36 g) golden raisins

1⅓ cups (315 ml) water

1 teaspoon (2.5 g) ground cinnamon

½ teaspoon (1.4 g) ground ginger

½ teaspoon (1.5 g) ground cloves

¼ teaspoon (0.7 g) ground nutmeg

½ cup (120 ml) lemon juice

2 teaspoons (10 ml) calcium water*

1¼ cups (250 g) sugar

3 teaspoons (9 g) Pomona's pectin powder

For information on how to prepare calcium water, refer to page 22.

1. If you are new to canning, or need a refresher, refer to chapter 1 (pages 12–41) for step-by-step guidance and additional information on how to safely can your marmalade. Once ready, proceed as follows.
2. Prepare your jars, lids, and bands; heat up your canner; and sterilize your jars.
3. Thoroughly wash the oranges. Peel the fruit and set aside peel from 1 orange, discarding the remaining peels. Remove and discard any seeds, excess white pith, or especially fibrous parts of the membrane from the flesh of both oranges. Finely chop the flesh of both oranges.
4. Using a paring knife, scrape off and discard the inner white part of the reserved peel. Slice the peel into thin strips, about 1-inch (2.5 cm) long.
5. In a large saucepan, combine chopped oranges, sliced peel, grated carrots, chopped pineapple, golden raisins, and the 1⅓ cups (315 ml) of water. Bring mixture to a boil. Reduce heat and simmer, covered, for 20 minutes, stirring occasionally. Remove from heat.
6. Measure 4 cups (946 ml) of the cooked fruit mixture (saving any extra for another use), and return the measured quantity to the saucepan. Add cinnamon, ginger, cloves, nutmeg, lemon juice, and calcium water. Mix well.
7. In a separate bowl, combine sugar and pectin powder. Mix thoroughly and set aside.
8. Bring fruit mixture back to a full boil over high heat. Slowly add pectin-sugar mixture, stirring constantly. Continue to stir vigorously for 1 to 2 minutes to dissolve pectin while the marmalade comes back up to a boil. Once the marmalade returns to a full boil, remove it from the heat.
9. **Can Your Marmalade:** Remove jars from canner and ladle hot marmalade into hot jars, leaving ¼ inch (6 mm) of headspace. Remove trapped air bubbles, wipe rims with a damp cloth, put on lids and screw bands, and tighten to fingertip tight. Lower filled jars into canner, ensuring jars are not touching each other and are covered with at least 1 to 2 inches (2.5 to 5 cm) of water. Place lid on canner, return to a rolling boil, and process for 10 minutes (adjusting for altitude if necessary). Turn off heat and allow canner to sit untouched for 5 minutes, then remove jars and allow to cool undisturbed for 12 to 24 hours. Confirm that jars have sealed, then store properly.

YIELD: 4 TO 5 HALF-PINT (8-OUNCE, OR 236 ML) JARS

KEEP IT EQUAL

If you have too much fruit and need to get rid of some to meet the required 4-cup (946 ml) quantity, be sure that you remove solids and liquids equally. This is very important in maintaining both the proper consistency and proper acidity of the final product. Don't pour off the liquid—instead, remove extra solids and liquids from the measuring cup one spoonful at a time, making an effort to remove liquid spoonfuls and solid spoonfuls in roughly equal quantities.

THREE-CITRUS MARMALADE

Winter is high season for citrus fruits, and they're so delicious and abundant at this time of year that sometimes it's hard to choose. Fortunately, with this recipe, you don't have to! Grapefruit, orange, and lemon—as well as honey—all contribute to this delicious, eclectic marmalade. Can you picture it with a bit of butter on a warm croissant? I can't imagine much better on a winter weekend morning.

4 medium lemons, divided

1 medium grapefruit (white or pink)

4 medium oranges

3 cups (710 ml) water

3 teaspoons (15 ml) calcium water*

1½ cups (510 g) honey

4½ teaspoons (13.5 g) Pomona's pectin powder

For information on how to prepare calcium water, refer to page 22.

GO ORGANIC!

Buying organic is always a good idea, but it's especially important when you're planning to use the peel of the fruit, as nonorganic produce may have been sprayed with pesticides or other chemicals that are nearly impossible to wash off. So choose organic citrus if you can for this recipe—it will make a difference!

1. If you are new to canning, or need a refresher, refer to chapter 1 (pages 12–41) for step-by-step guidance and additional information on how to safely can your marmalade. Once ready, proceed as follows.
2. Prepare your jars, lids, and bands; heat up your canner; and sterilize your jars.
3. Slice 1 of the lemons in half and squeeze out its juice, discarding seeds and peels. Set lemon juice aside.
4. Thoroughly wash all of the remaining fruit. Peel the fruit and set aside peel from 1 orange, 1 lemon, and ⅓ of the grapefruit, discarding the remaining peels. Remove and discard any seeds, excess white pith, or especially fibrous parts of the membrane from the flesh of all the fruit. Finely chop the flesh of all the fruit.
5. Using a paring knife, scrape off and discard the inner white part of the reserved peels. Slice the peels into thin strips, about 1-inch (2.5 cm) long.
6. In a large saucepan, combine chopped fruit, sliced peels, and 3 cups (710 ml) of water. Bring mixture to a boil over high heat. Reduce heat and simmer, covered, for 20 minutes, stirring occasionally. Remove from heat.
7. Measure 6 cups (1.4 L) of the cooked fruit (saving any extra for another use), and return the measured quantity to the saucepan. Add reserved lemon juice and calcium water and mix well.
8. In a separate bowl, combine honey and pectin powder. Mix thoroughly and set aside.
9. Bring fruit mixture back to a full boil over high heat. Slowly add pectin-honey mixture, stirring constantly. Continue to stir vigorously for 1 to 2 minutes to dissolve pectin while the marmalade comes back up to a boil. Once the marmalade returns to a full boil, remove it from the heat.
10. **Can Your Marmalade:** Remove jars from canner and ladle hot marmalade into hot jars, leaving ¼ inch (6 mm) of headspace. Remove trapped air bubbles, wipe rims with a damp cloth, put on lids and screw bands, and tighten to fingertip tight. Lower filled jars into canner, ensuring jars are not touching each other and are covered with at least 1 to 2 inches (2.5 to 5 cm) of water. Place lid on canner, return to a rolling boil, and process for 10 minutes (adjusting for altitude if necessary). Turn off heat and allow canner to sit untouched for 5 minutes, then remove jars and allow to cool undisturbed for 12 to 24 hours. Confirm that jars have sealed, then store properly.

YIELD: 6 TO 7 HALF-PINT (8-OUNCE, OR 236 ML) JARS

LEMON-CHERRY MARMALADE

Somewhere between a jam and a marmalade, this one might be my favorite marmalade yet. The addition of cherries adds a deep, intense sweetness, and the tartness of the lemon along with the mild bitterness of the peel temper that in beautifully. Spread this marmalade generously on crepes for a most spectacular breakfast treat!

2 pounds (910 g) sweet cherries*

5 medium lemons, divided

¼ cup (60 ml) water

4 teaspoons (20 ml) calcium water**

1 cup (200 g) sugar

3 teaspoons (9 g) Pomona's pectin powder

*Not sure how much fruit to purchase? See "Measuring Up!" on page 26.

**For information on how to prepare calcium water, refer to page 22.

PARING PEELS

Unlike other citrus fruits, lemon peels can be difficult to remove with your fingers. If you have trouble, carefully use a paring knife to slice the peel off.

1. If you are new to canning, or need a refresher, refer to chapter 1 (pages 12–41) for step-by-step guidance and additional information on how to safely can your marmalade. Once ready, proceed as follows.
2. Prepare your jars, lids, and bands; heat up your canner; and sterilize your jars.
3. Rinse cherries, remove stems, slice in half, and remove the pits. (For more information, see "Painless Pitting" on page 70.) Coarsely chop cherries and place in saucepan.
4. Slice 2 of the lemons in half and squeeze out their juice, discarding the seeds and peels. Divide the juice, reserving ¼ cup (60 ml) of the lemon juice for later use. Add any remaining quantity to the cherries.
5. Wash the remaining 3 lemons. Peel the fruit and set aside peels from 2 of the lemons, discarding the remaining peel. Remove and discard any seeds, excess white pith, or fibrous parts of the membrane from the flesh of all 3 lemons, then chop the flesh of all the lemons.
6. Using a paring knife, scrape off the inner white part of the reserved lemon peels and slice the peels into 1-inch (2.5 cm) long strips.
7. Add chopped lemons, sliced peels, and the ¼ cup (60 ml) water to the cherries. Bring fruit to a boil over high heat, reduce heat, and simmer, covered, for 12 to 15 minutes, or until peels are soft, stirring occasionally. Remove from heat.
8. Measure 4 cups (946 ml) of the cherry mixture (saving any extra for another use). Return the measured quantity to the saucepan. Add the reserved ¼ cup (60 ml) lemon juice and calcium water, and mix well.
9. In a separate bowl, combine sugar and pectin powder. Mix thoroughly and set aside.
10. Bring cherry mixture back to a full boil. Slowly add pectin-sugar mixture, stirring constantly for 1 to 2 minutes to dissolve pectin while the marmalade comes back up to a boil. Once the marmalade returns to a full boil, remove it from the heat.
11. **Can Your Marmalade:** Remove jars from canner and ladle hot marmalade into hot jars, leaving ¼ inch (6 mm) of headspace. Remove trapped air bubbles, wipe rims with a damp cloth, put on lids and screw bands, and tighten to fingertip tight. Lower filled jars into canner, ensuring jars are not touching each other and are covered with at least 1 to 2 inches (2.5 to 5 cm) of water. Place lid on canner, return to a rolling boil, and process for 10 minutes (adjusting for altitude if necessary). Turn off heat and allow canner to sit untouched for 5 minutes, then remove jars and allow to cool undisturbed for 12 to 24 hours. Confirm that jars have sealed, then store properly.

YIELD: 4 TO 5 HALF-PINT (8-OUNCE, OR 236 ML) JARS

MARGARITA MARMALADE

With plenty of south-of-the-border flair, and a generous kick of tequila, this grown-up marmalade is just plain fun. Laced with orange peels and loaded with limes, it's perfect on croissants or even mini cornbread loaves for a wedding shower brunch.

12 medium-size limes, divided

4 medium-size oranges

1½ cups (355 ml) water

3 teaspoons (15 ml) calcium water*

½ cup (120 ml) tequila

½ cup (120 ml) orange liqueur

2½ cups (500 g) sugar

4½ teaspoons (13.5 g) Pomona's pectin powder

*For information on how to prepare calcium water, refer to page 22.

1. If you are new to canning, or need a refresher, refer to chapter 1 (pages 12–41) for step-by-step guidance and additional information on how to safely can your marmalade. Once ready, proceed as follows.
2. Prepare your jars, lids, and bands; heat up your canner; and sterilize your jars.
3. Slice 2 of the limes in half and squeeze out their juice, discarding the seeds and peels. Divide the juice, reserving ¼ cup (60 ml) of the lime juice for later use. Then, set aside extra lime juice (if there is any) in a different container.
4. Wash the oranges. Peel oranges and remaining limes, and set aside peels from 2 of the oranges, discarding all remaining peels. Remove and discard seeds, excess white pith, or fibrous parts of the membrane from the flesh of the fruit. Chop the flesh of the fruit.
5. Using a paring knife, scrape off and discard the inner white part of the reserved orange peels. Slice the peels into thin strips, about 1-inch (2.5 cm) long.
6. In a large saucepan, combine chopped fruit, sliced peels, 1½ cups (355 ml) of water, and the extra lime juice, if there is any (*not* including the ¼ cup (60 ml) reserved juice). Bring mixture to a boil over high heat. Reduce heat and simmer, covered, for 20 minutes, stirring occasionally. Remove from heat.
7. Measure 5 cups (1.2 L) of the cooked fruit (saving any extra for another use), and return the measured quantity to the saucepan. Add calcium water, the ¼ cup [60 ml] reserved lime juice, tequila, and orange liqueur and mix well.
8. In a separate bowl, combine sugar and pectin powder. Mix thoroughly and set aside.
9. Bring fruit mixture back to a full boil over high heat. Slowly add pectin-sugar mixture, stirring constantly. Continue to stir vigorously for 1 to 2 minutes to dissolve pectin while the marmalade returns to a boil. Once it returns to a full boil, remove it from the heat.
10. **Can Your Marmalade:** Remove jars from canner and ladle hot marmalade into hot jars, leaving ¼ inch (6 mm) of headspace. Remove trapped air bubbles, wipe rims with a damp cloth, put on lids and screw bands, and tighten to fingertip tight. Lower filled jars into canner, ensuring jars are not touching each other and are covered with at least 1 to 2 inches (2.5 to 5 cm) of water. Place lid on canner, return to a rolling boil, and process for 10 minutes (adjusting for altitude if necessary). Turn off heat and allow canner to sit untouched for 5 minutes, then remove jars and allow to cool undisturbed for 12 to 24 hours. Confirm that jars have sealed, then store properly.

PARING PEELS

Unlike other citrus fruits, lime peels can be difficult to remove with your fingers. If you have trouble, carefully use a paring knife to slice the peel off.

YIELD: 6 TO 7 HALF-PINT (8-OUNCE, OR 236 ML) JARS

GRAPEFRUIT-HONEY MARMALADE

Inspired by the artisanal jam company Juniper Jammery's delicious Grapefruit Marmalade, this marmalade is different from others in this book in that it contains all fruit and no peel. It's delicious on muffins or toast, and it makes an excellent glaze for grilled vegetables or meats. That is, of course, if it doesn't get eaten up by the spoonfuls first—its luscious grapefruit flavor is intense and somewhat addictive.

6 large pink grapefruits

2 tablespoons (30 ml) lemon juice

3 teaspoons (15 ml) calcium water*

1 cup (340 g) honey

4 teaspoons (12 g) Pomona's pectin powder

*For information on how to prepare calcium water, refer to page 22.

1. If you are new to canning, or need a refresher, refer to chapter 1 (pages 12–41) for step-by-step guidance and additional information on how to safely can your marmalade. Once ready, proceed as follows.
2. Prepare your jars, lids, and bands; heat up your canner; and sterilize your jars.
3. Peel grapefruits and discard peels. Using your hands and working over a large bowl, separate grapefruit sections. Then, open up each section and pull the fruit out of the membrane, discarding the membranes. Collect the fruit and the resulting juice in the bowl, breaking fruit into small pieces as you work.
4. Measure 4 cups (946 ml) of the grapefruit-juice mixture (saving any extra for another use) and combine the measured quantity in a saucepan with lemon juice and calcium water. Mix well.
5. In a separate bowl, combine honey and pectin powder. Mix thoroughly and set aside.
6. Bring fruit to a full boil over high heat. Slowly add pectin-honey mixture, stirring constantly. Continue to stir vigorously for 1 to 2 minutes to dissolve pectin while the marmalade comes back up to a boil. Once the marmalade returns to a full boil, remove it from the heat.
7. **Can Your Marmalade:** Remove jars from canner and ladle hot marmalade into hot jars, leaving ¼ inch (6 mm) of headspace. Remove trapped air bubbles, wipe rims with a damp cloth, put on lids and screw bands, and tighten to fingertip tight. Lower filled jars into canner, ensuring jars are not touching each other and are covered with at least 1 to 2 inches (2.5 to 5 cm) of water. Place lid on canner, return to a rolling boil, and process for 10 minutes (adjusting for altitude if necessary). Turn off heat and allow canner to sit untouched for 5 minutes, then remove jars and allow to cool undisturbed for 12 to 24 hours. Confirm that jars have sealed, then store properly.

YIELD: 4 TO 5 HALF-PINT (8-OUNCE, OR 236 ML) JARS

MIX IT UP!

This marmalade has a tendency to separate in the jar after canning—this is normal. When you open the jar, simply mix it well before serving.

Chapter 7

ALTERNATIVE SWEETENERS

||||||||||||||||||||||||||||||||||||||||||||||||||||||||||||||||||||||||||||||||||||||||||||||||||||||

These days so many of us are trying to reduce our sugar consumption for any number of reasons—but we still want to enjoy delicious jams and jellies! Fortunately, Pomona's pectin is extremely versatile and can be used with just about any sweetener. This chapter is dedicated to jams and jellies that use *only* alternative sweeteners, such as agave nectar, stevia, and monk fruit.

Monk fruit and stevia are available in a variety of strengths and formulations, as they are blended with other ingredients to make them easier to measure and use as a replacement for sugar. For typical monk fruit sweetener blends, one teaspoon of the blend is equal in sweetness to one teaspoon of sugar. Stevia blends tend to be sweeter, with one teaspoon providing sweetness equal to two teaspoons of sugar. Monk fruit and stevia blends in these strengths are common and widely available, and this is what I have used in the developing these recipes. To ensure success with these recipes, purchase blends with this same level of sweetness.

MANGO-PINEAPPLE JAM

Both pineapples and mangoes are naturally very sweet, and because of this they are some of my favorite fruits to use in jams where I want to minimize the amount of sweetener I need to add. Pineapple provides an appealing tang, which balances out the sweetness beautifully and yields an absolutely delicious jam. Suffice it to say that this jam never lasts long in my refrigerator, as I typically eat it by the spoonful.

||||||||||||||||||||||||||||||||||||||||||||||||||||||||||||||||||||||||||||||||||||||||||||||||||||||||||||||||||||||||||||||||||||||||||||||||||||||||||

2 pounds (910 g) fully-ripe mangoes* (for more information, see "Do The Mango Mash!" below)

2 cups (330 g) finely chopped pineapple (for more information, see "Persnickety Pineapples!" on page 132)

⅓ cup (75 ml) lemon juice

3 teaspoons (15 ml) calcium water**

¾ cup (144 g) monk fruit sweetener blend

2½ teaspoons (7.5 g) Pomona's pectin powder

*Not sure how much fruit to purchase? See "Measuring Up!" on page 26.

**For information on how to prepare calcium water, refer to page 22.

||||||||||||||||||||||||||||||||||||||||||||||||||||||||||||||

DO THE MANGO MASH!

This recipe calls for mashed mangoes, so be sure that your mangoes are fully ripe and soft enough to mash. They'll also be much sweeter if they're fully ripe. If you simply can't wait for full ripeness, however, place peeled, pitted, chopped mango in a saucepan with ½ cup (120 ml) water. Simmer for 5 minutes to soften, and then mash mango by hand or puree in a food processor, being careful not to liquefy it. (There's no need to drain the water after cooking— simply mash or puree the mango mixture as is.)

1. If you are new to canning, or need a refresher, refer to chapter 1 (pages 12–41) for step-by-step guidance and additional information on how to safely can your jam. Once ready, proceed as follows.
2. Prepare your jars, lids, and bands; heat up your canner; and sterilize your jars.
3. Peel and pit mangoes, and then mash in a large bowl.
4. Measure 2 cups (330 g) of mashed mango (saving any extra for another use). Combine the measured quantity in a saucepan with the chopped pineapple, lemon juice, and calcium water. Mix well.
5. In a separate bowl, combine monk fruit sweetener and pectin powder. Mix thoroughly and set aside.
6. Bring mango-pineapple mixture to a full boil over high heat. Slowly add pectin–monk fruit sweetener mixture, stirring constantly. Continue to stir vigorously for 1 to 2 minutes to dissolve pectin while the jam comes back up to a boil. Once the jam returns to a full boil, remove it from the heat.
7. **Can Your Jam:** Remove jars from canner and ladle hot jam into hot jars, leaving ¼ inch (6 mm) of headspace. Remove trapped air bubbles, wipe rims with a damp cloth, put on lids and screw bands, and tighten to fingertip tight. Lower filled jars into canner, ensuring jars are not touching each other and are covered with at least 1 to 2 inches (2.5 to 5 cm) of water. Place lid on canner, return to a rolling boil, and process for 10 minutes (adjusting for altitude if necessary). Turn off heat and allow canner to sit untouched for 5 minutes, then remove jars and allow to cool undisturbed for 12 to 24 hours. Confirm that jars have sealed, then store properly.

YIELD: 4 TO 5 HALF-PINT (8-OUNCE, OR 236 ML) JARS

||||||||||||||||||||||||||||||||||||||||||||||||||||||||||||||

TRIPLE-BERRY JAM

When berries are abundant, and they are all so good that choosing is tough, this jam is the ticket! The combination of strawberries, blueberries, and raspberries takes advantage of the best of summer, and it offers something for everyone—all in one jam! This jam also allows for a little flexibility; if you like blackberries, substitute them in for some or all of the raspberries.

||||||||||||||||||||||||||||||||||||||||||||||||||||||||||||||||||||||||||||||||||||||||||||||||||||||||||||||||||||||||||||||||||||||||||||||||||||||||

¾ **pound (340 g) strawberries***

¾ **pound (340 g) blueberries***

¾ **pound (340 g) raspberries***

¼ **cup (60 ml) lemon juice**

2 **teaspoons (10 ml) calcium water****

½ **cup (96 g) stevia sweetener blend**

2 **teaspoons (6 g) Pomona's pectin powder**

Not sure how much fruit to purchase? See "Measuring Up!" on page 26.

**For information on how to prepare calcium water, refer to page 22.*

1. If you are new to canning, or need a refresher, refer to chapter 1 (pages 12–41) for step-by-step guidance and additional information on how to safely can your jam. Once ready, proceed as follows.
2. Prepare your jars, lids, and bands; heat up your canner; and sterilize your jars.
3. Rinse strawberries, remove stems, and mash in a large bowl.
4. Rinse blueberries, remove any stems, and mash in a large bowl.
5. Carefully pick through raspberries, removing stems and any damaged parts. Rinse raspberries only if necessary. Mash in a large bowl.
6. Combine all of the mashed berries and mix thoroughly. Measure 4 cups (946 ml) of the mashed berries (saving any extra for another use). Combine the measured quantity in a saucepan with lemon juice and calcium water. Mix well.
7. In a separate bowl, combine stevia sweetener and pectin powder. Mix thoroughly and set aside.
8. Bring berry mixture to a full boil over high heat. Slowly add pectin-stevia mixture, stirring constantly. Continue to stir vigorously for 1 to 2 minutes to dissolve pectin while the jam comes back up to a boil. Once the jam returns to a full boil, remove it from the heat.
9. **Can Your Jam:** Remove jars from canner and ladle hot jam into hot jars, leaving ¼ inch (6 mm) of headspace. Remove trapped air bubbles, wipe rims with a damp cloth, put on lids and screw bands, and tighten to fingertip tight. Lower filled jars into canner, ensuring jars are not touching each other and are covered with at least 1 to 2 inches (2.5 to 5 cm) of water. Place lid on canner, return to a rolling boil, and process for 10 minutes (adjusting for altitude if necessary). Turn off heat and allow canner to sit untouched for 5 minutes, then remove jars and allow to cool undisturbed for 12 to 24 hours. Confirm that jars have sealed, then store properly.

YIELD: 4 TO 5 HALF-PINT (8-OUNCE, OR 236 ML) JARS

ORANGE-MANGO MARMALADE

Marmalades typically include a lot of added sugar, as orange peels are a bit bitter and tend to be tastier when balanced out with a good dose of sugar. This recipe is an exception. In addition to the monk fruit sweetener that is used here in place of sugar, the sweet, ripe mangoes add a good deal of sweetness to this marmalade, making it a delicious, delightful, everyday breakfast treat.

|||||||||||||||||||||||||||||||||||||||||||||||||||||||||||||||||||||||||||||||||||||||||||||||||||||||||||||||||||||||||||||||||||||||||||||||||||||||||||||||||||||||||||||||||

4 medium-size oranges

2 cups (473 ml) orange juice

4 pounds (1.8 g) firm, ripe mangos*

½ cup (120 ml) lemon juice

3 teaspoons (15 ml) calcium water**

1¾ cups (336 g) monk fruit sweetener blend

4½ teaspoons (13.5 g) Pomona's pectin powder

Not sure how much fruit to purchase? See "Measuring Up!" on page 26.

**For information on how to prepare calcium water, refer to page 22.*

1. If you are new to canning, or need a refresher, refer to chapter 1 (pages 12–41) for step-by-step guidance and additional information on how to safely can your marmalade. Once ready, proceed as follows.
2. Prepare your jars, lids, and bands; heat up your canner; and sterilize your jars.
3. Wash the oranges thoroughly. Using a vegetable peeler, slice off long pieces of the exterior of the peels of two of the oranges, avoiding the inner white part. Then, using a chef's knife, slice these peels into thin strips about 1-inch (2.5-cm) long. Set aside.
4. Remove and discard any remaining peel, the white pith, and any seeds from these two oranges. Remove and discard all peel, pith, and seeds from the remaining two oranges. Finely chop the flesh of all of the oranges.
5. In a large saucepan, combine the chopped oranges, the sliced peels, and the orange juice. Bring the mixture to a boil over high heat. Reduce heat and simmer, covered, for 15 minutes, stirring occasionally.
6. While the oranges are cooking, peel, pit, and dice mangoes into uniform-size cubes, about ¾ inch (2 cm) each (for more information, see "Mango Madness" on page 63).
7. Add the diced mangoes to the oranges in the saucepan. Bring the mixture back to a boil, then reduce heat and simmer, covered, for another 2 to 4 minutes, until the mangoes are soft. Remove from heat.
8. Measure 6 cups (1420 ml) of the cooked fruit (saving any extra for another use) and return the measured quantity to the saucepan. Add lemon juice and calcium water and mix well.
9. In a separate bowl, combine monk fruit sweetener and pectin powder. Mix thoroughly and set aside.
10. Bring fruit mixture back to a full boil over high heat. Slowly add pectin–monk fruit sweetener mixture, stirring constantly. Continue to stir vigorously for 1 to 2 minutes to dissolve pectin while the marmalade comes back up to a boil. Once the marmalade returns to a full boil, remove it from the heat.
11. **Can Your Marmalade:** Remove jars from canner and ladle hot marmalade into hot jars, leaving ¼ inch (6 mm) of headspace. Remove trapped air bubbles, wipe rims with a damp cloth, put on lids and screw bands, and tighten to fingertip tight. Lower filled jars into canner, ensuring jars are not touching each other and are covered

with at least 1 to 2 inches (2.5 to 5 cm) of water. Place lid on canner, return to a rolling boil, and process for 10 minutes (adjusting for altitude if necessary). Turn off heat and allow canner to sit untouched for 5 minutes, then remove jars and allow to cool undisturbed for 12 to 24 hours. Confirm that jars have sealed, then store properly.

YIELD: 6 TO 7 HALF-PINT (8-OUNCE, OR 236 ML) JARS

GRAPE JELLY

Grape jelly is a childhood classic for sure; so many kids love peanut butter and jelly sandwiches! This jelly is a delicious version of the classic—with a whole lot less sugar. Agave nectar replaces the sugar in this recipe and, because grapes are naturally quite sweet, less added sweetener is necessary than in jams or jellies made with fruits that are more sour.

|||||||||||||||||||||||||||||||||||||||||||||||||||||||||||||||||||||||||||||||||||||||||||||||||||||||||||||||||||||||||||||||||||

4 pounds (1.8 kg) sweet black or purple grapes*

½ cup (120 ml) water

¼ cup (60 ml) lemon juice

4 teaspoons (20 ml) calcium water**

⅔ cup (158 ml) agave nectar

4 teaspoons (12 g) Pomona's pectin powder

*Not sure how much fruit to purchase? See "Measuring Up!" on page 26.

**For information on how to prepare calcium water, refer to page 22.

1. If you are new to canning, or need a refresher, refer to chapter 1 (pages 12–41) for step-by-step guidance and additional information on how to safely can your jelly. Once ready, proceed as follows.

2. Rinse grapes, remove stems, and combine in a saucepan with the ½ cup (120 ml) of water. Bring to a boil over high heat, reduce heat, and simmer, covered, for 8 to 10 minutes, stirring occasionally. Remove from heat and mash grapes.

3. Transfer mashed fruit to a damp jelly bag or layered cheesecloth, suspend over a bowl, and allow juice to drip until dripping stops—at least 2 hours. Discard fruit pulp or save for another use.

4. Prepare your jars, lids, and bands; heat up your canner; and sterilize your jars.

5. Carefully pour the juice out of its bowl and into another container, leaving the sediment in the bottom of the bowl. Discard the sediment. Measure 4 cups (946 ml) of the grape juice. (If you're short on juice, see "Where's the Juice?" on page 85 for more information.) Combine the juice in a saucepan with lemon juice and calcium water. Mix well.

6. In a separate bowl, combine agave nectar and pectin powder. Mix thoroughly and set aside.

7. Bring the juice mixture to a full boil over high heat. Slowly add the pectin-agave mixture, stirring constantly. Continue to stir vigorously for 1 to 2 minutes to dissolve pectin as the jelly comes back up to a boil. Once the jelly returns to a full boil, remove it from the heat.

8. **Can Your Jelly:** Remove jars from canner and ladle hot jelly into hot jars, leaving ¼ inch (6 mm) of headspace. Remove trapped air bubbles, wipe rims with a damp cloth, put on lids and screw bands, and tighten to fingertip tight. Lower filled jars into canner, ensuring that jars are not touching each other and are covered with at least 1 to 2 inches (2.5 to 5 cm) of water. Place lid on canner, return to a rolling boil, and process for 10 minutes (adjusting for altitude if necessary). Turn off heat and allow canner to sit untouched for 5 minutes, then remove jars and allow to cool undisturbed for 12 to 24 hours. Confirm that jars have sealed, then store properly.

YIELD: 4 TO 5 HALF-PINT (8-OUNCE, OR 236 ML) JARS

GINGERED BLUEBERRY-ORANGE PRESERVES

This delicious and decadent preserve is perfect for breakfast—and even better for dessert! Swirl it into yogurt, use it as a gorgeous topping for cheesecake, or simply put a dollop of it on top of vanilla ice cream. No one will even guess that it's low in sugar!

IIIIIIIIIIIIIIIIIIIIIIIIIIIIIIIIIIIIIIIIIIIIIIIIIIIIIIIIIIIIIIIIIIIIIIIIIIIIIIIIIIIIIIIIIIIIIIIIIIIIIIIIIIIIIIIIIIIIIIIIIIIIIIIIIIIIIIIIIIIIIIIIIIIIIIIIIIIIIIIIIII

2 pounds (910 g) blueberries*

3–4 oranges

1 tablespoon (8 g) peeled, finely grated ginger root

¼ cup (60 ml) lemon juice

2 teaspoons (10 ml) calcium water**

¾ cup (175 ml) agave nectar

2 teaspoons (6 g) Pomona's pectin powder

*Not sure how much fruit to purchase? See "Measuring Up!" on page 26

**For information on how to prepare calcium water, refer to page 22.

1. If you are new to canning, or need a refresher, refer to chapter 1 (pages 12–41) for step-by-step guidance and additional information on how to safely can your preserves. Once ready, proceed as follows.
2. Prepare your jars, lids, and bands; heat up your canner; and sterilize your jars.
3. Rinse blueberries and remove stems, then set aside. Wash oranges thoroughly. Using a vegetable peeler, slice off long pieces of the exterior of a couple of the peels, avoiding the inner white part. Then, using a chef's knife, slice these peels into very thin strips about 1-inch (2.5-cm) long. Repeat this process until you have accumulated ¼ cup (24 g) of thin strips of orange peel. Place the strips in a saucepan.
4. Slice oranges in half and squeeze out their juice until you have accumulated 1 cup (235 ml) of juice. Add the juice and the grated ginger root to the saucepan. Discard the remaining peels.
5. Cover the mixture and bring it to a boil over high heat. Reduce the heat and simmer, still covered, for 4 to 5 minutes, stirring occasionally, until orange peels are somewhat soft. Add the blueberries and return the mixture to a boil, stirring frequently. Reduce heat and simmer, still covered and stirring occasionally, for 1 to 2 minutes, or until the blueberries are soft and have released their juices. Remove pan from heat.
6. Measure 4 cups (946 ml) of the cooked mixture (saving any extra for another use). Return the measured quantity to the saucepan. Add lemon juice and calcium water and mix well. In a separate bowl, combine the agave nectar and pectin powder. Mix thoroughly and set aside.
7. Bring the blueberry mixture back to a full boil over high heat. Slowly add the pectin-agave nectar mixture, stirring constantly. Continue to stir vigorously for 1 to 2 minutes to dissolve pectin while the preserves come back up to a boil. Once the preserves return to a full boil, remove from heat.
8. **Can Your Preserves:** Remove jars from canner and ladle hot preserves into hot jars, leaving ¼ inch (6 mm) of headspace. Remove trapped air bubbles, wipe rims with a damp cloth, put on lids and screw bands, and tighten to fingertip tight. Lower jars into canner, ensuring that jars are not touching each other and are covered with at least 1 to 2 inches (2.5 to 5 cm) of water. Place lid on canner, return to a rolling boil, and process for 10 minutes (adjusting for altitude if necessary). Turn off heat and allow canner to sit untouched for 5 minutes, then remove jars and allow to cool undisturbed for 12 to 24 hours. Confirm that jars have sealed, then store properly.

YIELD: 4 TO 5 HALF-PINT (8-OUNCE, OR 236 ML) JARS

Chapter 8

PIE FILLINGS

If you enjoy making desserts, but often find yourself short on time, having ready-made pie filling on hand is the way to go! Typical pie filling (made with flour, cornstarch, or tapioca, for example) is not safe to can, but pie filling made with Pomona's pectin can be canned. It's easy to make and it's delicious!

With these pie fillings the fruit is left whole or cut into pieces, rather than being mashed, with the cooked fruit enveloped in a bit of jelled syrup. When making these pie fillings it's best to use fruit that is ripe but still very firm. Be sure to fully heat the fruit as quickly as possible, so it doesn't overcook. Also, make sure to stir the fruit very gently. These steps help the fruit retain its shape as much as possible, which is the goal when it comes to making pie filling. To ensure that your pie filling is processed for the correct amount of time, can your pie filling in pint jars or smaller—not in quarts.

So, get your hands on some fruit and get canning! With just a little extra effort now, you can stock your pantry shelves with an assortment of fillings for luscious fruit pies ready to make and enjoy at any moment!

APPLE-CRANBERRY PIE FILLING

Ah, autumn . . . crisp days with warm but waning sun, deeply colored leaves, and frost-tinged nights. And of course, apples and cranberries. In this pie filling these quintessential fall fruits are laced with warming spices, and when baked to piping hot in flaky pastry this pie filling says autumn like nothing else. Use firm, crisp apples in this recipe and heat them quickly so the apple slices retain their shape as much as possible.

½ pound (225 g) fresh cranberries*

1½ pounds (680 g) firm, crisp apples*

1¼ cups (250 g) sugar

1½ teaspoons Pomona's pectin powder

½ teaspoon cinnamon

¼ teaspoon nutmeg

¼ teaspoon cloves

½ cup (120 ml) unsweetened apple juice

¼ cup (60 ml) lemon juice

2 teaspoons (10 ml) calcium water**

Not sure how much fruit to purchase? See "Measuring Up!" on page 26.

**For information on how to prepare calcium water, refer to page 22.*

1. If you are new to canning, or need a refresher, refer to chapter 1 (pages 12–41) for step-by-step guidance and additional information on how to safely can your pie filling. Once ready, proceed as follows.
2. Prepare your jars, lids, and bands; heat up your canner; and sterilize your jars.
3. Rinse cranberries, then set aside.
4. Peel the apples, remove stems and cores, and cut into slices about ½ to ¾ inches (1.3 to 2 cm) thick. Set aside.
5. In a separate bowl, combine sugar and pectin powder. Mix thoroughly and set aside.
6. In a large saucepan, combine cranberries, apples, cinnamon, nutmeg, cloves, apple juice, lemon juice, and calcium water. Cover, then bring mixture to a boil over the highest heat, stirring frequently, until the liquid in the bottom of the pan is at a rolling boil, and the fruit itself is steaming hot. Continue to cook at a low boil, still covered, for 30 to 60 seconds, stirring frequently, until the fruit is just beginning to soften.
7. Bring the fruit mixture back to a full boil over high heat. Slowly add pectin-sugar mixture, stirring constantly. Continue to stir vigorously for 1 to 2 minutes to dissolve pectin while the pie filling comes back up to a boil. Once the pie filling returns to a full boil, remove the pan from the heat.
8. **Can Your Pie Filling:** Remove jars from canner and ladle hot pie filling into hot jars, leaving ½ inch (1.3 cm) of headspace. Remove trapped air bubbles, wipe rims with a damp cloth, put on lids and screw bands, and tighten to fingertip tight. Lower filled jars into canner, ensuring jars are not touching each other and are covered with at least 1 to 2 inches (2.5 to 5 cm) of water. Place lid on canner, return to a rolling boil, and process for 15 minutes (adjusting for altitude if necessary). Turn off heat and allow canner to sit untouched for 5 minutes, then remove jars and allow to cool undisturbed for 12 to 24 hours. Confirm that jars have sealed, then store properly.

YIELD: 2 PINT (16-OUNCE, OR 473 ML) JARS

STRAWBERRY-RHUBARB PIE FILLING

Here in Maine and other northern climates, spring is pretty sparse when it comes to locally available fruit. Rhubarb and strawberries are some of the first fruits of the season, usually making a welcome appearance in late spring. As much anticipated harbingers of the summer season, it's no surprise that tangy rhubarb and lusciously sweet strawberries are a favorite combination when it comes to pie.

1 pound (455 g) strawberries*

1 pound (455 g) trimmed rhubarb stalks*

1⅓ cups (273 g) sugar

2½ teaspoons (7.5 g) Pomona's pectin powder

¼ cup (60 ml) water

2 tablespoons (30 ml) lemon juice

2 teaspoons (10 ml) calcium water**

*Not sure how much fruit to purchase? See "Measuring Up!" on page 26.

**For information on how to prepare calcium water, refer to page 22.

1. If you are new to canning, or need a refresher, refer to chapter 1 (pages 12–41) for step-by-step guidance and additional information on how to safely can your pie filling. Once ready, proceed as follows.
2. Prepare your jars, lids, and bands; heat up your canner; and sterilize your jars.
3. Rinse strawberries and remove stems. If the strawberries are very large, slice each berry in half. Set aside.
4. Rinse rhubarb, slice stalks lengthwise into strips, then cut into small pieces—approximately ¾-inch (2-cm) dice. Set aside.
5. In a separate bowl, combine sugar and pectin powder. Mix thoroughly and set aside.
6. In a large saucepan, combine rhubarb, water, lemon juice, and calcium water. Cover, then bring the mixture to a boil over the highest heat. Cook at a low boil, still covered but stirring frequently, for about 1 minute, until the rhubarb has softened somewhat. Add the strawberries, then return the mixture to a boil over the highest heat, stirring frequently, until the liquid in the bottom of the pan is at a rolling boil, and the strawberries are steaming hot. Continue to cook at a low boil, still covered, for 30 to 60 seconds, stirring frequently, until the strawberries are just beginning to soften and release their juices.
7. Bring the fruit mixture back to a full boil over high heat. Slowly add pectin-sugar mixture, stirring constantly. Continue to stir vigorously for 1 to 2 minutes to dissolve pectin while the pie filling comes back up to a boil. Once the pie filling returns to a full boil, remove the pan from the heat.
8. **Can Your Pie Filling:** Remove jars from canner and ladle hot pie filling into hot jars, leaving ½ inch (1.3 cm) of headspace. Remove trapped air bubbles, wipe rims with a damp cloth, put on lids and screw bands, and tighten to fingertip tight. Lower filled jars into canner, ensuring jars are not touching each other and are covered with at least 1 to 2 inches (2.5 to 5 cm) of water. Place lid on canner, return to a rolling boil, and process for 15 minutes (adjusting for altitude if necessary). Turn off heat and allow canner to sit untouched for 5 minutes, then remove jars and allow to cool undisturbed for 12 to 24 hours. Confirm that jars have sealed, then store properly.

YIELD: 2 PINT (16-OUNCE, OR 473 ML) JARS

PEACH-GINGER PIE FILLING

Peaches are the quintessential summer fruit—straight-up juicy, sweet, and gorgeous—and inside a flaky pie crust they are equally spectacular. In this pie filling, grated ginger root adds a subtle heat and complexity that gracefully balances the full-on sweetness of the peaches.

2¾ pounds (1.2 kg) ripe but very firm peaches*

1 cup (200 g) sugar

2 teaspoons (6 g) Pomona's pectin powder

2 teaspoons (5.4 g) peeled, finely grated ginger root (for more information, see "Grate That Ginger!" on page 125)

¼ cup (60 ml) lemon juice

2½ teaspoons (12.3 ml) calcium water**

Not sure how much fruit to purchase? See "Measuring Up!" on page 26.

**For information on how to prepare calcium water, refer to page 22.*

1. If you are new to canning, or need a refresher, refer to chapter 1 (pages 12–41) for step-by-step guidance and additional information on how to safely can your pie filling. Once ready, proceed as follows.

2. Prepare your jars, lids, and bands; heat up your canner; and sterilize your jars.

3. Peel and remove pits from peaches. Then, cut peaches into slices about ½ to ¾ inches (1.3 to 2 cm) thick. Set aside. (For more information, see "How to Skin a Peach" on page 58.)

4. In a separate bowl, combine sugar and pectin powder. Mix thoroughly and set aside.

5. In a large saucepan, combine peaches, grated ginger root, lemon juice, and calcium water. Cover, then bring mixture to a boil over the highest heat, stirring frequently, until the liquid in the bottom of the pan is at a rolling boil, and the fruit itself is steaming hot. Continue to cook at a low boil, still covered, for 30 to 60 seconds, stirring frequently, until the peaches are just beginning to soften and release their juices.

6. Bring the peaches back to a full boil over high heat. Slowly add pectin-sugar mixture, stirring constantly. Continue to stir vigorously for 1 to 2 minutes to dissolve pectin while the pie filling comes back up to a boil. Once the pie filling returns to a full boil, remove the pan from the heat.

7. **Can Your Pie Filling:** Remove jars from canner and ladle hot pie filling into hot jars, leaving ½ inch (1.3 cm) of headspace. Remove trapped air bubbles, wipe rims with a damp cloth, put on lids and screw bands, and tighten to fingertip tight. Lower filled jars into canner, ensuring jars are not touching each other and are covered with at least 1 to 2 inches (2.5 to 5 cm) of water. Place lid on canner, return to a rolling boil, and process for 15 minutes (adjusting for altitude if necessary). Turn off heat and allow canner to sit untouched for 5 minutes, then remove jars and allow to cool undisturbed for 12 to 24 hours. Confirm that jars have sealed, then store properly.

YIELD: 2 PINT (16-OUNCE, OR 473 ML) JARS

BLUEBERRY-MAPLE-VANILLA PIE FILLING

Straight-ahead blueberry pie is delicious, but this pie filling provides a delightful twist on the classic. The addition of maple and vanilla, combined with fresh blueberries, is luscious and truly dreamy. It makes an incredible pie that's perfect to bring along on a summertime picnic. If you prefer a more classic blueberry pie flavor profile, however, feel free to omit the vanilla bean and substitute white sugar for the maple sugar.

2 pounds (910 g) blueberries*

1 cup (152 g) maple sugar

2 teaspoons (6 g) Pomona's pectin powder

5 tablespoons (75 ml) lemon juice

2 teaspoons (10 ml) calcium water**

1 vanilla bean

*Not sure how much fruit to purchase? See "Measuring Up!" on page 26.

**For information on how to prepare calcium water, refer to page 22.

1. If you are new to canning, or need a refresher, refer to chapter 1 (pages 12–41) for step-by-step guidance and additional information on how to safely can your pie filling. Once ready, proceed as follows.
2. Prepare your jars, lids, and bands; heat up your canner; and sterilize your jars.
3. Rinse blueberries and remove stems, then set aside.
4. In a separate bowl, combine maple sugar and pectin powder. Mix thoroughly and set aside.
5. In a large saucepan, combine blueberries, lemon juice, and calcium water. Then, using a paring knife, slice the vanilla bean in half lengthwise and scrape out the seeds into the saucepan. Add the vanilla bean pod as well. Cover, then bring mixture to a boil over the highest heat, stirring frequently, until the liquid in the bottom of the pan is at a rolling boil, and the fruit itself is steaming hot. Continue to cook at a low boil, still covered, for 30 to 60 seconds, stirring frequently, until the blueberries are just beginning to soften and release their juices.
6. Bring the blueberries back to a full boil over high heat. Slowly add pectin–maple sugar mixture, stirring constantly. Continue to stir vigorously for 1 to 2 minutes to dissolve pectin while the pie filling comes back up to a boil. Once the pie filling returns to a full boil, remove the pan from the heat. Using tongs, carefully remove the vanilla bean pod and discard.
7. **Can Your Pie Filling:** Remove jars from canner and ladle hot pie filling into hot jars, leaving ½ inch (1.3 cm) of headspace. Remove trapped air bubbles, wipe rims with a damp cloth, put on lids and screw bands, and tighten to fingertip tight. Lower filled jars into canner, ensuring jars are not touching each other and are covered with at least 1 to 2 inches (2.5 to 5 cm) of water. Place lid on canner, return to a rolling boil, and process for 15 minutes (adjusting for altitude if necessary). Turn off heat and allow canner to sit untouched for 5 minutes, then remove jars and allow to cool undisturbed for 12 to 24 hours. Confirm that jars have sealed, then store properly.

YIELD: 2 PINT (16-OUNCE, OR 473 ML) JARS

GO FOR THE REAL THING!

There is a lot of imitation maple syrup on grocery store shelves. Be sure to get the real thing. Check the label—what you're looking for is 100 percent pure maple syrup. It's a bit pricey, but it's so worth it!

PEAR-CARDAMOM PIE FILLING

Luscious, subtle, and complex all at the same time, I consider pears the pinnacle autumn fruit. This pie filling highlights their brilliance beautifully with cardamom adding a touch of earthy spiciness. Tucked into a flaky pie crust, it makes a lovely dessert on a crisp autumn day. Use pears that are ripe but still very firm, so the pears will retain their shape as much as possible.

IIIIIIIIIIIIIIIIIIIIIIIIIIIIIIIIIIIIIIIIIIIIIIIIIIIIIIIIIIIIIIIIIIIIIIIIIIIIIIIIIIIIIIIIIIIIIIIIIIIIIIIIIIIIIIIIIIIIIIIIIIIIIIIIIIIIIIIII

3 pounds (1.4 kg) ripe but very firm pears*

¾ cup (150 g) sugar

1½ teaspoons Pomona's pectin powder

1 teaspoon ground cardamom

¼ cup (60 ml) lemon juice

2 teaspoons (10 ml) calcium water**

*Not sure how much fruit to purchase? See "Measuring Up!" on page 26.

**For information on how to prepare calcium water, refer to page 22.

1. If you are new to canning, or need a refresher, refer to chapter 1 (pages 12–41) for step-by-step guidance and additional information on how to safely can your pie filling. Once ready, proceed as follows.

2. Prepare your jars, lids, and bands; heat up your canner; and sterilize your jars.

3. Peel and remove cores from pears. Then, cut pears into slices about ½ to ¾ inch (1.3 to 2 cm) thick. Set aside.

4. In a separate bowl, combine sugar and pectin powder. Mix thoroughly and set aside.

5. In a large saucepan, combine pears, ground cardamom, lemon juice, and calcium water. Cover, then bring mixture to a boil over the highest heat, stirring frequently, until the liquid in the bottom of the pan is at a rolling boil, and the fruit itself is steaming hot. Continue to cook at a low boil, still covered, for 30 to 60 seconds, stirring frequently, until the pears are just beginning to soften and release their juices.

6. Bring the pears back to a full boil over high heat. Slowly add pectin-sugar mixture, stirring constantly. Continue to stir vigorously for 1 to 2 minutes to dissolve pectin while the pie filling comes back up to a boil. Once the pie filling returns to a full boil, remove the pan from the heat.

7. **Can Your Pie Filling:** Remove jars from canner and ladle hot pie filling into hot jars, leaving ½ inch (1.3 cm) of headspace. Remove trapped air bubbles, wipe rims with a damp cloth, put on lids and screw bands, and tighten to fingertip tight. Lower filled jars into canner, ensuring jars are not touching each other and are covered with at least 1 to 2 inches (2.5 to 5 cm) of water. Place lid on canner, return to a rolling boil, and process for 15 minutes (adjusting for altitude if necessary). Turn off heat and allow canner to sit untouched for 5 minutes, then remove jars and allow to cool undisturbed for 12 to 24 hours. Confirm that jars have sealed, then store properly.

YIELD: 2 PINT (16-OUNCE, OR 473 ML) JARS

Resources

Where Can I Buy Pomona's Universal Pectin?

At the time of publication, Pomona's is available at most Whole Foods stores and Sprouts stores, as well as many other natural food or health food stores and co-ops in the United States and Canada. You can also find it at some farmstands, some smaller independent grocery stores, and a growing number of health-conscious conventional food stores, such as Wegmans (in New York State and the mid-Atlantic) and QFC (in the Northwest). Pomona's is also available at Williams-Sonoma, both in their stores and online.

Online shoppers can also order both the 1-ounce (28 g) boxes and in bulk directly from the Pomona's website (www.pomonapectin.com), or a variety of other online sellers, including Amazon.

The list of stores where Pomona's is available is constantly growing and changing. Check the Pomona's website to contribute to the effort to crowd-source the stores that carry Pomona's, or to see whether a store is listed in your area.

Where Can I Find More Information About Pomona's?

1. Go to the website, www.pomonapectin.com, where you will find:

    - An extensive list of frequently answered questions (FAQs).
    - An updated list of where to find Pomona's Pectin.

2. Thoroughly read the directions that come in the box with Pomona's. You'll find recipes and directions for making No-Cook Freezer Jam, as well as directions for making more jam with artificial sweeteners.

3. Sign up for the Pomona's e-newsletter, *Jam Notes*, either from the website or from the Pomona's Facebook page. *Jam Notes* is published three times a year: February, June, and September.

4. Like or follow Pomona's on Facebook, Instagram, and Pinterest.

If you have questions about pectin or want to tell us about your experience with Pomona's, feel free to write a comment, send us an email, or give us a call.

Contact:
Green Link LLC
P.O. Box 4408
Oakhurst, CA 93644
(559) 760-0910
info@pomonapectin.com

For quick product information or simple jamming questions, email us at info@pomonapectin.com.

For product information or jamming questions requiring involved answers, please call our JAMLINE at (559) 760-0910.

Acknowledgments

There are so many people who have contributed to this project. First off, I want to thank Mary Lou Sumberg, Connie Sumberg, and Paul Rooney of Pomona's Pectin for the opportunity to write this book—I am tremendously grateful. You have been wonderful partners, and I sincerely appreciate your confidence in me and support throughout the project. Also, thanks to all of the jam makers who submitted recipes for inclusion in this book.

This book has been all-consuming for the past many months, and writing it would not have been possible for me without the help and support of so many people. Thank you to my good friend Margaret Hathaway who gave me encouragement and much-needed advice when I was first considering this project, and to my friend Sharon Kitchens for her publicity assistance and guidance. Thank you to my brother and sister-in-law, John and Lisa Carroll, and their family for their recipe ideas. Thank you to my stepmother Ann Carroll for all her creative recipe ideas, as well as lots of fresh herbs from her garden. I am especially grateful to all of my parents, Chick and Ann Carroll and Connie and Etienne Perret, for their ever-present love and support, and for the many hours they spent caring for our boys while I was writing, developing recipes, and canning like mad. And, thank you to the various food preservers I have learned from and who have inspired me over the years—in particular, my mother-in-law, Terry Redlevske, and University of Maine Cooperative Extension Educator, Kathy Savoie.

My biggest thank you goes to my husband Ben and our two young sons. Connor and Ian, thank you so much for your patience, resilience, and understanding of my general lack of availability during the process of writing this book, and for your ever-present energy, vitality, inquisitiveness, and love. And Ben, I am deeply grateful for you, and for all that you do for me and for our family. I know that this project has also required a lot of you. Thank you for picking up the slack in so many areas of our lives while my attention was focused on this book—my deepest thanks for your unwavering love, encouragement, and support through it all.

About the Author

Allison Carroll Duffy has been growing and preserving food for over 20 years. She is a Master Food Preserver, trained through the University of Maine Cooperative Extension, and also holds a masters degree in gastronomy from Boston University. She teaches food preservation classes, has written about food for various publications including the *Boston Globe* and *Backpacker* magazine, and has made television and video appearances as a jam-making and canning guest expert on shows such as *Vegan Mashup*, *Mature Lifestyles*, and *207 Kitchen*. Allison lives on several acres in mid-coast Maine with her husband, their two teenage boys, a puppy, and many chickens. You can follow her canning and preserving adventures at www.canningcraft.com.

Index